The Year of Dating Myself

The Year of Dating Myself

HOW MY SOLO TOUR HEALED
MORE THAN JUST MY HEARTBREAK

ABBY ROSMARIN

Copyright © 2025 by Abby Rosmarin.

All rights reserved. Except for brief passages quoted in newspaper, magazine, radio, television, or online reviews, no part of this book may be reproduced in any form or by any means, electronic or mechanical, including photocopying or recording, or by information storage or retrieval system, without permission in writing from the publisher.

Published in the United States by Viva Editions, an imprint of Start Midnight, LLC, 221 River Street, Ninth Floor, Hoboken, New Jersey 07030.

Cover design: Jennifer Stimson Design
Cover image: iStock / xmocb
Mountain illustraition: Oleksandr Poliashenko
Text Design: Westchester Publishing Services

First Edition.
10 9 8 7 6 5 4 3 2 1

Trade paper ISBN: 978-1-63228-099-2
E-book ISBN: 978-1-63228-117-3

For Salem, my baby boy

CONTENTS

xi   Introduction

1   **September (the previous year)**

3   Prologue: I'm Done/How Did I Get Here?

9   **Part I: January**

11   Chapter 1: In Another Life

15   Chapter 2: The Solo Tour

19   Chapter 3: Kismet and Impulse

23   Chapter 4: My Childhood Toys

31   Chapter 5: Platonic Love

35   **Part II: February**

37   Chapter 6: Regrets, Genetics, and Apologies

43   Chapter 7: Valentine's Day

53   Chapter 8: Ice-Skating

59   **Part III: March**

61   Chapter 9: Corrective Experiences

67   Chapter 10: Intimacy, Robbery, Infancy

71   Chapter 11: Solo, and Dueling

CONTENTS

77	**Part IV: April**
79	Chapter 12: Thunder and Lightning
85	Chapter 13: Inner Teen
87	Chapter 14: Lady Luck Is on My Side
97	Chapter 15: The Theater
103	**Part V: May**
105	Chapter 16: Co-opt
109	Chapter 17: On Hammocks, On Quiet, On Empty
111	Chapter 18: Salem
117	Chapter 19: Mothering
123	Chapter 20: Back to the Start
129	**Part VI: June**
131	Chapter 21: Alone, with Cats
135	Chapter 22: Laugh Where You Cried
139	Chapter 23: Pride
143	**Part VII: July**
145	Chapter 24: Reassurance
149	Chapter 25: The Longest Week
155	Chapter 26: Philadelphia
159	Chapter 27: Ongoing
163	Chapter 28: Threat

CONTENTS

167   **Part VIII: August**

169   Chapter 29: It's Okay to Suck

173   Chapter 30: Something's Fixed, Something's Broken

179   Chapter 31: Timing, Pacing

183   Chapter 32: Return

191   Chapter 33: Blended

195   **Part IX: September**

197   Chapter 34: Taking Care

203   Chapter 35: An Itch You Can't Scratch

209   Chapter 36: Pop Quiz

215   Chapter 37: Shattered

219   Chapter 38: Communicate

223   Chapter 39: Weight

227   **Part X: October**

229   Chapter 40: Interrogate

237   Chapter 41: Hiking

245   Chapter 42: Shine

251   Chapter 43: Undertake

CONTENTS

257 Part XI: November

259 Chapter 44: Magic

267 Chapter 45: Tour's End

269 Chapter 46: Freedom

275 Part XII: December

277 Chapter 47: Vacancy

283 Chapter 48: Homecoming

289 Chapter 49: Investment

293 Chapter 50: Light and Dark

301 Chapter 51: Layers

309 Chapter 52: Bigger than Me

315 Part XIII: January (the following year)

317 Epilogue: What Now?

329 Afterword/Acknowledgments

Introduction

This book took me one year to write.

Technically, eleven months, for the first draft. I was one month into the "Year of Dating Myself" experiment when I decided I wanted to document my journey in real time. Writing has been my saving grace. Even at my lowest points, I knew that if I could find the words, I was going to be okay. Writing is not only how I process, but how I find insight. Words have been the crowbar, prying open unexamined areas, exposing hidden feelings to fresh air. I knew writing about my experience would provide a layer of healing that nothing else ever could—but I didn't realize just how much. I was connecting dots that had previously been in isolation. My words set the stage for the more subtle wounds to step onto. My words were a comforting embrace when the bigger wounds were overwhelming.

But perhaps the biggest healer was going back, reading through the first draft (which, unedited, was more than 125,000 words), and watching how my writing evolved. I watched a woman who was still trying to make heads or tails of what she'd just gone through become a woman who stood in her own story. Editing that first draft (particularly, editing down the word count) felt like a conversation with my past self, letting her know that everything was going to be all right. (For reference, the final word count of this book is half of that original number.)

That being said, if it feels like the wording changes as the year progresses, it's because I changed as the year progressed. I was dating myself, but, in a sense, I was also dating countless different versions of myself throughout the year.

INTRODUCTION

As a note, all names in this book are changed, as are identifying details. I knew the only way I could talk about everything with unfettered honesty was to disconnect from the people I was writing about. Writing with their names was not unlike invoking their very being to read over my shoulder, anxiously curious what I was going to say about them. Everything has been written as accurately as possible. However, some details were condensed or omitted to let the story breathe. (The first draft did no such thing. Hence the 125,000 words.)

You'll notice that most of my exes mentioned do not have a name; that was done purposely. For the well-meaning men who've been in my life, may it shield them from scrutiny. For the men who hurt me the most: I know oblivion would be an even worse fate than scrutiny. May any name for them—even aliases—be lost to the sands of time.

September
(the previous year)

Prologue: I'm Done/ How Did I Get Here?

My then-boyfriend sat on the other end of the video call, stone-faced.

I felt hollowed out. His volatility had been bad that day. I'd been trying, once again, to explain to him why his behavior wasn't okay. The conversation was headed in the same direction as all of our previous talks. The only difference was that he'd suddenly changed his approach. He started insisting that yelling, "I see how it is! I'm the bad guy! It's all my fault!" was just him acknowledging blame and apologizing.

"No," I'd said, moments before crying. "You know that's not what you were doing."

"Really, that's what I was doing. I was simply apologizing because I realized I was to blame," he replied.

That was the moment I hung my head back and started to cry. My brain felt fuzzy, like I couldn't decipher what was up and what was down. My heart was exhausted and in agony. My knuckles had gone white from how hard I'd been clutching to the Prince Charming that I once knew. I had nothing left in me but sorrow—and there was nothing left to do but cry.

"Well, what do you want me to do?!" my then-boyfriend shouted through the phone, interrupting my tears.

A wild thing happens when the only thing you have left is sorrow—and the other person makes it unsafe to feel that sorrow:

You officially have *nothing* left.

And that means nothing left to *lose*.

My tears stopped. My emotions retreated. Something overcame me, and I looked at my then-boyfriend with a robotic coldness that made him uneasy.

"I don't have to do this in front of you," I stated.

"No, I was just asking if there was something I could do," he stammered, "to make you feel supported."

"No, no. That's not what happened, at all . . . ," I replied slowly, my voice detached. I felt like a passenger in my own body. "Yeah. I don't have to do this in front of you."

And I hung up.

The next day, I got a text from him, asking if we could talk to discuss "where we go from here." But I was already taking down our photos—because, as I eventually told him that day, where we went from there was *nowhere*. Because we were done.

I was done.

I sunk chin-deep into the water—a mountainous bubble bath surrounded by candles; the only way I knew how to keep the crushing darkness from consuming me. I'd just seen my ex-boyfriend in person for the first time since I had ended things the week before—and hopefully for the last time ever. He'd dropped off my belongings and I'd sobbed in his arms, and for a moment I'd forgotten what he'd put me through.

That night, the weight of it all was unbearable. It really was *over*. My fairytale really had been a nightmare, and there'd be no heroic turnaround in the third act. My Prince Charming was gone—and it didn't matter that he technically never existed. I was left in pieces, while he gallivanted off like nothing happened.

How did I get here?

Not with the relationship. Not with the bubble bath. But with *me*.

How did I get here?

It was my fifth romantic nightmare in a row. Each one had been worse than the previous. After each fallout, I'd promised to stay single, only to immediately jump into another disastrous relationship.

How did I let myself fall this far? How did I become this kind of person? How could I swear I'd learned my lesson and then immediately prove I'd learned nothing?

I had no answers.

Perhaps it was for the best. Any answers from that night would've been forgotten. Soon after that night in my bathtub, I'd learn that breaking up with my ex was just the start of things. I wasn't prepared for what came next. I wasn't prepared for the disorienting world of being an internet personality's ex, with thousands of people watching. I wasn't prepared for his efforts to keep me from talking about my experience. I wasn't prepared for women contacting me, finally revealing what had been going on behind my back. I wasn't prepared to learn that he'd lied about everything—absolutely *everything*. I wasn't prepared to call the relationship what I'd known to be true for months: abusive.

My only saving grace during that time were my friendships. One of those friends—Georgia—gave me a priceless invitation that December:

Did I want to join her for a New Year's trip to Arches National Park?

THE YEAR OF DATING MYSELF

I answered by doing something that would've terrified past versions of myself: I bought a round-trip ticket to Las Vegas for a vacation that I had only weeks to prepare for.

Something clicked during that trip with Georgia.

As I hiked the snowy trails, I realized something: it'd been only three months since I left my last relationship, and yet it was the longest that I'd been single since I was nineteen years old.

I'd been relationship hopping for nearly half my life.

I'd been frantically dating since my marriage ended, with no room to breathe, let alone process. I I swore off dating only as a superficial reaction against pain. All it took was a hint that my Prince Charming had arrived, and I'd abandon my convictions.

I'd wanted my happily ever after—and, when each attempt instead added another sad chapter, I only grew more desperate.

At the risk of victim blaming, my personality rang the dinner bell for men with dubious motives. I'd then serve myself up—and be dismayed that they actually went ahead with carving into me. There had been a glaring blind spot, and I was finally noticing it. I'd sworn off dating for many reasons, but none of them were truly *about* me, let alone *for* me.

I stumbled into that realization the way one inevitably stumbles into insight in nature. But what exactly was I supposed to do with that insight? Swear off dating, *for real*? What would make it any different than my previous attempts?

That New Year's Eve, on the drive home from a cold but fruitful day at Arches, sitting passenger side and scrolling through my phone, I had a moment of kismet. A promotional email from my favorite band sat in my inbox. They were touring again and playing locally in the spring. I went to look for tickets, only to find that the show was nearly sold out. A scattering of single seats was all that remained.

I almost exited the ticket website when a question popped into my mind: *when was the last time I'd been to a concert by myself?*

The answer was never. I'd never been to a concert by myself.

When I thought about it, I hadn't done *much* by myself, period.

I purchased one of the solo seats. I was going to go to the concert—by myself. I was going to do something *alone*, for once.

I was going to take myself out.

At that moment, something clicked.

Still in the passenger seat of Georgia's rented SUV, I went from the confirmation page for my ticket to my notes app. I started listing things I wanted to do in the new year: places I wanted to visit, activities I wanted to try, and long-distance friends I needed to see. I wrote down abstract and concrete goals.

As the last day of the year wound down, a plan was in place. I needed to be away from the dating world, yes, but that was just a surface-level action. What I truly needed was to be reintroduced to the very person I kept ignoring for the sake of my promised fairytale.

What I needed was to reignite a love that never truly got a chance to blossom in the first place.

What I needed was to get better acquainted with the person I lost, time and time again, for the sake of whoever I was dating.

What I needed was to take all that energy that I'd spent overly investing in romance and reinvest it.

What I needed to do was date myself.

Part I: January

Chapter 1: In Another Life

If the multiverse theory is true, then there's a version of me who never even started the Year of Dating Myself. She instead repeated her patterns before her plans could metaphorically get off the ground—while she waited for her plane to literally get off the ground.

I boarded my flight back from my New Year's trip with Georgia when a man with a handsome face and a gentle demeanor sat down next to me. He gave me a quick smile, slid his bag under the seat, and began fiddling with the console in front of him.

"Are there any outlets?" he asked me.

"I'm not sure," I said, looking around with him. "There are USB ports up here, at least," I said as I tapped on the console screen directly in front of me.

"Ah, yeah, but this wouldn't fit," he replied as he held up a cord with a different connector. "That's why I'm just looking for an outlet. It's easier."

I looked down and saw a dim red light at the base between seats.

"Ah, eureka," I deadpanned, pointing to the outlets.

"Thank you! I appreciate it," he plugged in his charger then added, "I wish I could use those USB ports up here. It would be a lot easier."

"Seriously!" I replied, and we had a quick back and forth about technology.

As we talked, I felt something surge through me—and it was enough for me to let the conversation gently die. In an alternative universe, there's a version of me who took that surge as her green light—her go-ahead to strike up more conversation, to add in a flirty smile, to delude herself into thinking it's empowering to "see where things go."

(But, if the multiverse theory is true, there are also universes where that man is in a relationship—or where the plane crashes, or the sun explodes, or World War III breaks out at that very moment. Perhaps it's for the best that I don't dwell too much on alternative universe versions of me.)

The version of me from *this* universe, however, understood that the feeling wasn't a green light, but a warning siren.

What was that feeling?

I'd gotten *giddy*.

I'd felt a welling of hope. I had the start of butterflies in my stomach.

I knew exactly what came next. That was when I'd used those butterflies to throw myself into the deep end of potential—and ignore anything to the potential's contrary. That was where I'd fill in blanks before learning the answers. It was the proverbial tide pulling back before the tsunami hits—and, for once, I wasn't just standing on the beach, awestruck that the water receded.

The first time I told that story, people assumed that I was imagining the worst of that man—that I had stopped talking to him because I thought he was scum. But despite what I'd recently gone through, I hadn't assumed anything negative.

But I also didn't assume anything positive, either.
I simply didn't know him.
And that was the point.

I'd previously let those butterflies dictate everything. I had treated dating like a game of fill-in-the-blanks, where most of the story was already written out and I was just looking for the missing nouns and prepositions. I'd learned the hard way that "and they lived [adverb] ever after," can create wildly different sentences.

I didn't interact with him for the rest of the flight. Not even a goodbye when it was time to deboard. By the time I stood up to grab my carry-on from the overhead compartment, he was already walking down the aisle. I could say I lost sight of him by the time I exited the plane, but that would give the impression that I was looking for him in the first place. Who he was as a person wasn't my focus, anyway. He was long gone, but what he represented stuck by my side, heavier than the overstuffed duffle bag slung over my shoulder. A small interaction had proven to be a large mirror—and I was weary of what it reflected.

I spent the next few days expanding the list for the Year of Dating Myself.

I contacted my friends from around the country; friends that I either hadn't seen since they moved away or newfound online friends that I'd technically never met, at least not in person. I mapped out—figuratively and literally—where I wanted to go, and when.

Maintain your 4.0 for spring, summer, and fall semesters, I wrote. I was halfway through my master's in clinical psychology. It'd been pure luck that my personal life hadn't affected my grades—but it was undeniable that it had affected my education.

Dating myself had to include reprioritizing school.

THE YEAR OF DATING MYSELF

I thought about all the activities I wanted to try and others I missed doing.

Where is there a giant Ferris wheel? I asked in my notes. *What does it take to do a helicopter ride?*

Improve my Spanish, I wrote down. *Befriend a murder of crows.*

Something big for Valentine's Day, I wrote with a heaviness in my chest.

I paused, smirked, and deleted the line.

Do something big for Valentine's Day, because fuck that douchebag, I wrote instead.

Sometimes levity is what keeps you from drowning.

I wrote *get your childhood toys back,* with a gravity that eclipsed everything else. I didn't dare try to lighten that one with humor.

I looked at my list and smiled. Had I continued my previous dating pattern, I'd already be in a new relationship. My pattern had previously been so blatant that my friend Lindsey had recently checked in on me, cautiously making sure I wasn't "giving love another chance," yet again.

Instead, I had a page and a half of ideas, goals, and possibilities to explore.

I was breaking the pattern.

All it took was a rapid-fire series of bad relationships, with the last one nearly breaking my sanity. No biggie.

But, in a way, that's what it had to take.

We can't cross certain thresholds until we've met the necessary threshold. Sometimes we have to get our maximum fill of mistakes before we can start to learn from them. It had to get to that point for me. It was not the first time that I had to hit rock bottom before I'd take the climb back out seriously. But what mattered was that I was on the climb. I had plans for the year—and, while my list was meticulous enough to suggest some predictability, I truly had no idea what was in store for me.

Chapter 2: The Solo Tour

I truly believe that we cross paths with people for reasons bigger than we can understand.

My last relationship had happened under a unique set of circumstances. Before my ex became just that, he was someone from the internet—someone whose content I'd been consuming when he slid into my direct messages, telling me how incredible I was. By that point, I thought I knew him, through that image of a shy, affable man that he'd immaculately crafted online. Parasocial bonds are stealthy like that. He lived several hundred miles from me, but it didn't seem to matter. What's a little distance when you've found the man of your dreams?

Leaving the relationship had created a different set of unique circumstances—one that I wouldn't wish on anyone. His fans—the ones who'd also bought into his affable image—were ready to skewer me for anything that might contradict the man that they "knew." But this unique world also gave rise to people who actually knew my ex-boyfriend in real life reaching out to me. Other ex-girlfriends, former friends, and those who'd worked with him in the local arts scene: people who wanted to share their experiences with me to simultaneously find their validation, as well as my own. The interactions typically lasted for as long as it took to compare notes. A few, however, evolved from commiseration to companionship.

Stella was one of those friendships. She was once friends with my ex and had reached out to me. From there, a friendship formed—the kind of friendship that blossoms because you're both on parallel paths in life. I told her about my plans for my Year of Dating Myself. She told me that she was planning to do something similar: it was going to be the year when she went out and did things on her own, without worrying about having a boyfriend to do it with.

She named her plan the "Solo Tour."

"That's an amazing title," I told her. She extended it for me to use as well.

Perhaps on my own, I would've planned out a decent year. But having Stella as my cocaptain brought everything to another level.

We began bouncing ideas off each other. We became each other's cheerleaders.

We even had commemorative denim jackets.

Stella had a knack for painting designs on clothing. She'd already made herself a Solo Tour jacket. She planned to list out her adventures on the sleeves like a rock band listing their tour stops.

She offered to make one for me, and I graciously accepted.

Before she mailed me the jacket, Stella sent me a time lapse video of her painting the design. In the video, a majestic profile of a woman's face took shape, a woman with beautiful, sparkling gray hair. Her eyes were closed, as if taking something in.

It was perfect.

I was blown away when the jacket showed up at my doorstep. The video didn't do the painting justice. I put the jacket on and it felt like an ethereal hug. I started using both terms when talking about the year. I told people, "This is the 'Year of Dating Myself,' my 'Solo Tour.'" Both titles were important to me.

In an ironic twist, the Solo Tour title also served as a reminder that I wasn't doing it alone.

A common saying is if you lose the relationship, but find yourself, it's a win. I'd lost the relationship and found not only myself, but at least one incredible friend as well.

While it didn't feel like it back then, in retrospect, I'd made off like a bandit, in the end.

Chapter 3:
Kismet and Impulse

How my Valentine's Day plans came together felt like divine timing—or the ingenuity of advertising.

Do something big for Valentine's Day, because fuck that douchebag—my comedic alternative to an otherwise heavy line.

My previous Valentine's Day had been, on the surface, fine: my new boyfriend, my long-distance charmer, had ordered takeout to my house and we'd spent the night together over video chat.

It was in what I learned, later on, that tainted the night.

Some of the women who reached out after I left him were the women he was also two-timing during our relationship—including a local woman from his art community. He had told that woman that she didn't need to worry about me, because I was just a friend. He'd promised her that our Valentine's Day date—in fact, our entire relationship—wasn't real. He was only doing it to further his online career. Unbeknownst to me, my Prince Charming was busy in his castle, working behind my back.

I knew I needed some kind of corrective measure for my solo Valentine's Day. I needed new memories to steamroll over the previous year. The funny thing about opportunity is that sometimes

THE YEAR OF DATING MYSELF

it doesn't knock so much as it enters the room just as you're glancing over.

One night in January, I'd pulled up a calming video on my phone—my nightly ritual to stave off insomnia—when an advertisement filled my screen.

I typically ignored the ads. This one, however, caught my eye.

Hamilton, the musical, was coming to Boston.

I sat up, grabbed my phone, and clicked the link.

Not only was *Hamilton* coming to Boston, but they had a show on Valentine's Day. I immediately looked for tickets. The Valentine's Day show was nearly sold out—a few solo seats and nothing else. A disappointment for anyone looking for a date night with their partner.

But, for those looking for a date night with *themselves?*

I found one seat, orchestra center, with a drastically marked down price.

I had a plan for Valentine's Day.

I purchased my seat and felt giddiness wash over me.

I was going to take myself into the city for brunch, and then walk about the town. I'd do a romantic dinner for one before I'd finally get to see *Hamilton*.

I was so jazzed that it took another hour before I could even attempt to fall asleep. But it was worth it. I had stumbled into a perfect set of plans. It was the kind of Valentine's date I deserved. I hadn't had a truly thoughtful Valentine's Day since my marriage—and, even then, our last Valentine's Day rang like two people desperate to make a broken bell chime smoothly again.

I thought about the Valentine's Day I had spent with a man who had already dumped me once to reunite with his ex-wife (and was only a few months away from doing it again). I had my thoughtful gifts and greeted him at the door in red lingerie.

He gave me a card.

"I hope you know how cared about you are," he'd written at the bottom—a watered down mimic of how I'd say to him, "I hope you know how loved you are."

I took the card with grateful glee—because I still prided myself on being "low maintenance" back then. But I now know that it had never been the case with me.

I was just someone who believed that it was the only way she could be loved.

She emptied herself while expecting nothing in return—and it attracted men who were happy to get everything for nothing. Those days were over. I knew I deserved consideration. I deserved to have a Valentine's Day that made me feel special. I deserved to have a night on the town, to be in the presence of someone who was truly invested in me.

And that was exactly what I was going to get.

At least, that was the plan. I went to sleep that night, not realizing I'd soon learn just how terribly plans can go awry.

Chapter 4: My Childhood Toys

Much like my Year of Dating Myself, the decision to retrieve my childhood toys was a slow rumble until something clicked into place. The rumble started in my therapy sessions—sessions where we'd conceptualize my childhood wounds as a little girl version of me. The rumble intensified at a gift shop just outside Arches National Park, seeing miniature versions of the plastic horses I had as a child.

My toys were a tender subject for me. My childhood toys sat in boxes in my childhood home's basement—a house I hadn't been to in nearly a decade—not since my father had passed away. In my early twenties—and soon after his Parkinson's diagnosis—my father had become obsessed with clearing out my childhood bedroom. He wanted to turn the room into his miniapartment, away from his wife—my mother.

I obliged. I drove down and packed up a room that had been frozen in time since my adolescence, taking all my young adult books and CDs. My father quickly moved in, placing a minifridge where my bookshelves had been and a TV where my boombox once sat. A few years later, with his health rapidly fading, my father went into the storage spaces built into the eaves and pulled out all

THE YEAR OF DATING MYSELF

my early childhood toys that were stored in there. He demanded that I come down and pick up those items as well. By that point, I'd given up any hope of a healthy relationship with him. I was sick of how he treated my mother—openly ridiculing her, yet still expecting her to be his nurse and maid. A woman who'd been navigating her Alzheimer's diagnosis for years but had to take care of my father instead.

I was sick of his antics—and clearing out forgotten storage space felt like one more antic. Much to his fury, I didn't oblige. I kept my distance. I I saw my father only one more time: when he was comatose and hours away from death. Alone in his hospital room, I said, "I forgive you," to his unconscious body and didn't mean it. I stayed for the memorial and then never returned home again.

During that same time, I was unceremoniously dropped by my very first therapist. I didn't return to therapy for years—not until I swore off dating for the second time and realized I needed help.

With my new therapist, we used Eye Movement Desensitization and Reprocessing (EMDR) to process my parents' abuse. We made progress with memories of my father, but we stalled out with memories of my mother. It was apparently easy enough to process my father firing a gun just above my head or smacking me with the full force of his body weight—but my mother? That was going to be tougher. No matter what we did, my stomach still churned, remembering the way her face went beet red when she'd get inches from mine.

"It's interesting," my therapist observed, after a while. "We've hit way more roadblocks with your mother than we ever did for your father, but you also seem to have more of a protective attitude about your mother."

"I guess I feel bad for her," I said.

"I wonder if it's more than that," said my therapist. "The way you talk about her, it has me guessing that, in the beginning, you had a secure and healthy attachment with her. But then something changed."

I thought about my mother, a woman who was thirty-five when I was born. I thought about my mom's diagnosis of early onset Alzheimer's in her late fifties, when brain scans showed decaying gray matter. I thought about when symptoms of Alzheimer's can first appear. I thought about how my mother was forty-five when I entered the fifth grade. I thought about the sudden emotional regression I had in the fifth grade, the kind that merited weekly sessions with a school counselor.

What if her outbursts, her peculiar behavior—what if it could be attributed to a brain disease that wouldn't be detected for another decade?

At that moment, something clicked into place.

"That little girl version of you is feeling safe enough to return home," my therapist said, when I told her about my plans. "She wants her stuff back."

I made two important calls that week. The first call was to my younger brother, asking if it would be all right to come visit, to see him and my mother, and to *finally* take home my childhood toys. The second call was to my doctor's office, scheduling an appointment to discuss genetic testing for early onset Alzheimer's.

I drove to my hometown on a dreary January afternoon. My phone's Bluetooth periodically lost its connection with my car. Each time it reconnected, my phone alerted me as to how long it would take to drive to my house.

Even my phone was tempting me to turn back.

I didn't know what I was expecting when I arrived in my hometown. I knew a lot had changed—my sleepy suburban town had been outfitted into a commuter hub, a consequence of Boston's

THE YEAR OF DATING MYSELF

skyrocketing cost of living—but I was only unsettled by the fact that nothing was unsettling. The familiar sights were familiar. The unfamiliar was just that: unfamiliar. I detoured to the beach, standing in the bitter ocean breeze until my skin couldn't stand it anymore.

Something caught in my throat once I entered my old neighborhood. Everything looked like miniature replicas of themselves. The houses—all Cape-style homes, one-and-a-half-story structures with a design so simple it looked like a child had drawn them—felt tinier than I remembered.

I pulled up to my childhood home, feeling a weird, disconnected sense of homecoming. I rang the doorbell and heard the muffled barks of my brother's dog. I heard my mother's voice soon after. My brother opened the door. My brother was my mother's caretaker, and had ownership of the house; a deserved trade-in for looking after her. I stepped into the living room and greeted the timid dog, whose cast-down eyes gave hint to what he'd gone through before being rescued. My mother sat in an overstuffed loveseat across the room, smiling vacantly.

"And who might you be?" she asked.

"I'm . . . Abby."

"Oh!" My mom's face lit up. "I have an Abby! She was named after Abigail Smith Adams!"

I smirked. My entire life, I'd been told that I wasn't named after Abigail Adams. Apparently that was one of the more innocent lies of my childhood.

"Mom, this *is* your Abby," my brother chimed in.

"Oh! *My* Abby!" My mom's face lit up again. "*My* Abby. This is *my* Abby . . ."

She repeated her words, over and over again, like a child remembering arithmetic. It would've sounded no different, had she been saying, "Five times five is twenty-five."

26

I followed my brother to the basement. There, waiting for me, were my childhood belongings. A lone plastic horse lay situated on top of a cardboard filing box. My heart both rose and sank. There was one of my beloved plastic horses, like the ones that the Arches gift shop had miniatures of. But what if that had been the only one that survived?

"I can help bring these to the car," my brother offered.

Slowly and methodically, we carried the boxes out of the basement and into my hatchback. I opened each box, peeking inside before carrying them out. Dolls, teddy bears, children's books . . . I eventually opened one box and sighed with relief.

There, in a tangled mess, were the rest of my horses.

Miraculously, we were able to fit everything into my car. I then followed my brother around as he gave me a tour of the house. He wanted to show off all the home improvement projects he'd done, and the changes he made. I did my best to listen along, but I couldn't stop myself from opening closet doors, or saying things like, "I don't remember the kitchen being this small!" I wasn't trying to be condescending. I felt like I'd been placed in an optical illusion. I was realizing for the first time just how cramped everything was.

I joined my younger brother as he walked his dog. I studied the neighborhood as if I were going to draw a map of it later. My brother told me about who'd moved out, who'd passed away, who were still living with their parents. It made me think of all the children our age who'd lived in that neighborhood—and how they'd all been friends with each other, but not with us. When I was nine years old, I learned that houses were not soundproof by hearing my parents' screaming from three houses down. I was considerably older when I finally put two and two together:

We had no neighborhood friends growing up because we were "*that* house."

THE YEAR OF DATING MYSELF

I stayed for dinner. As my brother cooked in the kitchen, I attempted to have some conversation with my mom. I anchored myself by focusing on my brother's dog, who came to trust me enough for belly rubs. I talked superficially. I spoke about graduate school like I didn't care if I dropped out tomorrow. I'd learned the hard way to create emotional distance when talking to my mom. At some point, I gestured to a photo of her on top of a mountain.

"I actually know what mountain you're on, based on what's in the background," I said. "I climbed that mountain."

My parents had once summited all of New Hampshire's tallest mountains, back at the start of their relationship. Those who were Four Thousand Footer Club members were people who had completed such a task. I'd accomplish the same feat, a few years after my father died.

I paused and added: "I'm a 4,000-Footer member now too."

"Oh, yes. Hiking is really good," she said.

I felt my stomach drop. I abandoned the topic entirely.

My brother came out, serving dinner on the coffee table by my mom's loveseat. I helped clear the table afterwards, silently noting how the table that was once for family dinners had come to serve as a countertop for medication. As I said my goodbyes, I gave my mom a gentle hug, as if too tight of a squeeze would break her. I got into my car and sat in shock at how calm I was.

"I'm glad I did this," I said in a voice message to Stella. "I think I've made peace with who my mom is, and what my childhood was like."

I truly believed what I was saying. I believed it as I drove out of my hometown and back onto the highway. I believed it as I drove through Boston and north of the city.

I believed it, right up until I felt inspired to start playing music from Peter, Paul and Mary.

Peter, Paul and Mary were a staple of my childhood. My mom once told me that "Leaving on a Jet Plane" was my first favorite song.

But, then again, who knows if that were the truth? My mom had also told me that I wasn't named after Abigail Adams.

She'd also told me that the scars on my forehead were from when I tripped and fell into a table corner, multiple times.

Regardless, this much was true: when "Leaving on a Jet Plane" started playing, the veneer of calm shattered.

I cried like a child, unabashed, unadulterated, and loud. I cried through the entirety of *Album 1700*, and I cried some more as I played it again.

I cried as I crossed state lines. I cried as I pulled into my driveway. I cried as I parked in my garage.

I turned off my car. I stayed in my seat. I kept crying.

I'd done a lot of work in my therapy sessions, using that conceptualized child version of myself to heal. My therapist had been working dutifully beside me, using parts work therapy and EMDR to help my nervous system finally understand what my logical brain knew: that I didn't live in that environment anymore, and that "little child" me was safe. That little girl—the one who grew up in a house where the screams could be heard halfway across the neighborhood—finally had her stuff back. Symbolically and literally, and finally, she'd moved out of that house.

I'd spent so much time dissecting my past, pinpointing every time I'd acted from that wounded child side of me, every time "little girl me" was at the helm of the ship, deciding which men I'd cling to, the things I'd put up with, and the reasons to stay.

In the Year of Dating Myself, I'd been able to show "little girl me" that I'd become the parent that she deserved. She was safe now, and—with her toys, her books, all the things that spoke to her more than any trick from a therapist could—she finally believed it.

THE YEAR OF DATING MYSELF

She was safe—and in that safety, she was able to fully grieve what she'd been through.

That was what the tears were for. She was grieving, and I was grieving alongside her.

On that drive home, with my beloved plastic horses, teddy bears, and childhood books surrounding me, I'd taken a major step forward in my healing journey—a journey that I worried my last relationship had unraveled irreconcilably.

I was exhausted when the tears stopped and I finally got out of my car. But I still moved every box out of my car and into my house. It was as if the idea of leaving those toys in the car, just as they were finally back in my possession, was unimaginable.

We'd come this far. It was time they came home, fully, too.

Chapter 5: Platonic Love

The following weekend, I caught a flight to Pennsylvania.

Britt was a long-distance friend, and another reminder that some people are destined to come into your life at the exact time you need them. We'd both known of the other long before we officially became friends. We existed on the peripheries of each other's online communities, and once we realized that the other was just as excited for friendship, our bond tumbled headfirst. Britt became one of my best friends right as my last relationship went from a fairytale to a nightmare. She witnessed in real time the mental gymnastics I did, trying to justify my then-boyfriend's increasingly problematic behavior, finding new ways to blame myself for it. She watched it until she became the person calling me, the day after one of his blowups. She held a gentle, compassionate space for me as I sobbed for hours on video chat.

My January trip to see her had been confirmed before the Solo Tour had even begun. I'd purchased my plane ticket to see Britt a week before I bought my ticket to join Georgia on her New Year's trip.

I knew why I'd gravitated to travel, long before the Year of Dating Myself had a name. The only travel I'd previously done was

THE YEAR OF DATING MYSELF

with a romantic partner. I had attempted my first solo trip, that infamous September, just weeks before I'd left my last relationship. It was like I knew, even then, that the only way to salvation was to branch out on my own. But my trip to Québec City was sullied by what was going on back home. I spent my days frantically walking the streets of Old Québec, never fully outpacing the cloud of dread that surrounded me. I spent my nights in my room, pulling tarot cards, trying to make sense of things, ignoring the constant hum of heartbreak.

It was why I couldn't wait to fly out to see Britt, and why I impulsively agreed to Georgia's trip. I needed to try again with travel. My first attempt had floundered *that* badly.

My weekend with Britt was quick and impactful and full and fun. Britt had worried about how she'd entertain me—but there was a gentle yet constant reminder that such entertainment wasn't needed. We spent most of the weekend in conversation, discussing everything in our lives, easily laying bare our souls because we knew beyond a shadow of a doubt that our souls were the same. We spent time together like it was something we did every weekend. It felt so normal and so natural that a part of me was confused when it was time to fly back.

Why do I have to get on a plane and fly thousands of miles away from here? That makes no sense! Clearly, I live just down the street!

I remembered how people viewed our friendship, once they found out we were both queer women. A bisexual fairytale: two women, two best friends, after a lifetime of dating primarily men, realizing that the people they were supposed to be with were each other.

I understood the intention, but it still made me sad. Not because I wasn't going to live up to their expectations, but because it was a reminder of how society viewed love. Somewhere along the line,

32

society lost the knowledge that sometimes the deepest, most intimate love you will ever experience is platonic.

The previous year had been a crash course on the need for friendship, especially when romantic love was a source of pain. It was my platonic companions who gave support as I watched my world crumble. It was my longtime friends who saved my birthday when my then-boyfriend had upended it. It was my platonic love that kept my feet on the ground when I barely knew my up from down. It was my friendships that helped me find lucidity through the fog that my ex's mind games had created.

And again, a budding long-distance friendship was helping me find clarity where the long-distance romance had created muddying—particularly around the idea that I was high maintenance and impossible to please. It was clear from my time with Britt that I didn't need much. I just needed the genuine presence of people I felt safe with.

It was all I was asking for in my romantic relationship too. My ex had just distorted it into, "everyday has to be like a vacation for you!"

An abuser's greatest trap is made by reframing genuine investment as a demand for the moon on a silver platter. But a key to freedom is in friends that not only invest in you, but remind you that you *do* deserve the moon. And the stars.

Part II: February

Chapter 6: Regrets, Genetics, and Apologies

"I'm having a hard time with this feeling," said my friend Toni.

Toni, a longtime friend who'd recently moved to Wyoming, had called me one morning.

"I feel like I'm to blame for my marriage falling apart," she continued. "I didn't know how to fully show up for a relationship. But once I finally knew how to do that, it was wasted on abusive jackasses who took advantage of it."

"I wish I didn't know that feeling so well," I replied as I commiserated with her. "I wish I knew what would help in moments like this."

Toni and I had lived parallel lives. We'd married young to our college sweethearts—men with kind hearts and giving spirits. Like Toni, I brought all my unpacked childhood trauma into my marriage with Gabe like the worst kind of wedding dowry. We both knew there had been a fundamental incompatibility in our respective marriages, regardless of what we'd brought to the table. But logic doesn't quiet the voice that says it was *your* damage, *your* trauma, that ruined it all.

Both of our marriages ended amicably and mutually, with husbands transitioning into friends. Through a trial by fire, both Toni and I eventually unpacked our trauma and found avenues for healing. We finally became the people we knew we could be. But those people were then wasted on men who used our ability to communicate, to give the benefit of the doubt, against us. Toni and I wondered if we could ever trust romantic love again after that.

In that worry, we overanalyzed the one relationship in which we'd been treated well. We turned to a place where rational thought had no voice. Where it didn't matter that Gabe and I thrived as friends; where, the more we disentangled our lives from each other, the better we got along. If our husbands had been kind and the marriage still failed, that must mean it was our fault.

I knew that it was going to be one of the harder elements of the Year of Dating Myself. I knew the year would be more than just buying myself flowers. I knew I had relationship-hopped to avoid certain aspects of my life.

At that moment, I felt like someone who'd stopped running from the tsunami and turned to face it head-on. The gesture only looks brave until the waves hit and the person is thrashed underwater. I was going to have to sit with the years of pain that I'd been running from—pain that compounded with each failed relationship.

And it was going to feel as excruciating as drowning.

I met with my doctor in early February to talk about genetic testing.

As my mother's biological daughter, I was considered as high risk as it gets, and there were three specific proteins that would seal my fate. My friends were on standby during that doctor's appointment, but I knew I was going to be okay. I'd spent most of my life with a nagging voice that told me that I'd end up just like my mother. It was the reason I hated how I looked when I scowled (it was my mother's scowl). It was also the reason I hated my flyaway hairs (those same flyaways would stick out during my mother's episodes). I'd been plagued by a great unknowing. I was going to get answers—and, through those answers, a more concrete plan.

But I also knew I wouldn't have any answers coming straight out of that appointment. And I didn't. My doctor told me that he'd research which labs were available, and what they charged. However, as I'd eventually learn, it wasn't going to be as simple as finding a lab and swabbing my cheek. A large part of me already knew that. But a small part of me was hoping it would be.

That's the thing with hope. It's like the child, sitting awake on Christmas morning, convinced that Santa had brought them everything they'd asked for.

And who has the heart to tell them otherwise?

I received a disarming friend request a few days later. Truth be told, it was hard to tell exactly when this person sent the request; it was on a social media platform that I rarely used. But, as soon as I logged in, I got a pop-up notifying me that someone was trying to add me as a friend.

A man I never thought I'd hear from again.

In a movie, this would've been the part where my heart dropped—where time stood still as I held my breath.

But that's not what happened.

I just felt an uneasy sadness.

The man who had dumped me twice to reunite with his ex-wife wanted to be my *friend*.

After our final breakup, I blocked his number. I blocked him on every platform in which I knew he had a profile, save the accounts I wasn't aware existed.

Like the one I rarely used.

THE YEAR OF DATING MYSELF

Our last interaction had not been a pleasant one. He'd called me to say that he and his ex-wife were, once again, going to try to make it work.

"You could probably tell this was happening in the background . . ." he began.

What a funny way of saying "behind my back."

For the first time in our relationship, I yelled at him. I let out everything that I'd held my tongue on. I sharpened the edges of the truth and slashed him with it. My spine grew two times bigger while my heart shrunk five that afternoon. I ended the call and never heard from him again.

Word through the grapevine was that the marriage attempt didn't even last a month.

I spent a long time feeling furious with him. God knows what I would've said, had he tried to reach out during that time. God knows how vicious I would've been. But eventually, something cooled in me. I was able to see the version of me who dated him— the one who lacked boundaries, who knew from the beginning that she'd always live in the shadow of his ex-wife. The one who saw the red flags and took it as a sign to love him harder. The one who took him back, despite knowing that his ex-wife was still in his peripheral vision. The one who thought a card with an indirect reminder that she was "cared about" was more than what she deserved.

I'd grown a lot since then—and I imagined he had as well. A lot can happen after exiting someone's life. I'd wondered if he sent the friend request in hopes we could talk. Perhaps he even wanted to apologize. He might've also seen my name as a suggested friend and clicked the request button without much thought. Fleshing out either narrative would have driven me insane, so I placed both down and deleted his request.

He might've wanted to apologize. He might've wanted to get back together. He might've wanted to send an unsolicited dick pic.

All I knew was that had I accepted the request—if I'd opened the door even *that* much to let him back into my life—I would've begun filling in the blanks on his behalf, *once again.*

In some ways, I already was.

What happened, happened. He might've needed to give an apology, but I didn't need to receive it. I knew that he wasn't a bad man. He'd commodified me while pining for another woman, but that didn't make him a villain. He might've needed reconciliation, but I needed for that door to stay closed. For the first time in our entire dynamic, I wasn't going to sacrifice myself because of what *he* might need.

When I was younger, I couldn't block people. No matter how terrible they were. It felt too harsh, too final. It took way too long to realize that, when I kept the door to communication open, I stayed on the lookout for an apology. I was hoping for the moment when they'd realize their misdeeds.

In hoping, the wounds that those people had created were left to fester.

Sometimes the most freeing thing we can do is lock the door behind us.

Chapter 7: Valentine's Day

I had a lot of plans for Valentine's Day.

I'd been giddy about them all month. I didn't have work or class, which gave me the entire day to make the holiday as special as possible.

However, my plans didn't include getting pulled over the day before.

I was on my way to class when a police cruiser flashed their lights behind me. I pulled over and opened my glove compartment to grab my registration. It was at that moment I realized that I hadn't renewed my car's registration.

I was frustrated with myself; I was usually so on the ball about renewing. I figured that was why I was pulled over. It was an honest mistake, and hopefully the officer would see that. A female officer approached my window and asked if I had my license and registration.

"That's the funny part," I said with a self-conscious chuckle. "It's just now that I realized I didn't renew last year."

"Hey, that's okay. I just want to run it through the system, just to make sure everything's good," she said.

THE YEAR OF DATING MYSELF

I handed over my license and my expired registration, but there was something off in her words, and I couldn't shake the feeling it gave. The feeling only amplified as the minutes dragged on, as five minutes became ten, which became fifteen. It amplified further when a second cruiser pulled up.

"Do you know a 'Victoria Smith?'" A second police officer, also a woman, approached my passenger door.

"No . . . why?"

"I've never really seen this happen before, but it looks like while your vehicle was unregistered, someone registered with your vanity plate."

My heart sank.

I'd had my vanity plate for as long as I'd had my car. It held tremendous, sentimental significance—and I couldn't believe my luck that such a configuration had been available. However, if a person fails to renew their registration, their vanity plate configuration becomes available again. In the four months that my car had not been registered, someone else had snatched it up.

"I'm not sure what to do next," said the first police officer. "It's clear that your car was registered to these plates, but they're not currently, not anymore. Technically, we're supposed to take the plates . . ."

A feeling washed over me and it was enough to tip the scales. I could no longer hold back what had been building up within me. During the time that the officer had run my license and called for backup, something had dawned on me. I'd always been diligent about registration. I'd even get my car inspected a month earlier than needed, to give myself time for any repairs. How could I have missed something as important as my registration?

The answer came at me hard, but not as hard as the memories attached with it.

In my state, car registration expires on your birth month.

What was happening in my birth month—the month of September—the year prior?

I was fighting for my emotional life.

From August onward, I'd been dealing with the crescendo of my last relationship. At the end of September, I'd been pushed past my limit, but given a moment of clarity—and I used that clarity to leave. When I had started to vaguely talk online about what I'd gone through, I'd watched him launch a multifront retaliation. Then I started to find out about the cheating and just how much of my relationship had been a lie.

Gee, I wonder why car registration had slipped my mind.

"Do you have to be somewhere?" the first officer asked.

"Class," I said, and my voice broke. I could tell she caught my voice breaking.

"Hold on, let's see what we can do," she said.

She and the second officer walked back to their vehicles, and I began to sob.

There were layers to that cry. My sentimental plates were no longer mine. I was going to miss class. I was officially that car on the side of the road with two cop cars behind it, the kind of situation that people stare at and wonder what the driver possibly could've done to be in that much trouble.

But—above all else—I'd been sent back in time.

All the pain, the confusion, the anxiety, the dread, the anger, the rage, the betrayal, and the heartbreak . . . all of it came rushing back.

And I could not stop crying about it.

"Hey, it's okay, don't cry," the first officer said when she returned. "So, it really is just a case of someone else just registered that vanity plate. I know, what were the odds?"

Her tone was completely different. She was being jovial. The gesture was kind and made me want to cry even more.

THE YEAR OF DATING MYSELF

"This was a total freak accident," she continued. "We just put it in the system that the registration has expired, and we're letting you off with a warning. Call the town clerk tomorrow and they'll be able to help you get new plates. We won't be taking the plates. But hold onto this registration! I hope you're not too late to class."

"Thank you, truly," I said, gripping my expired registration. "I promise I'm fine. I'm just remembering why I forgot to register."

"These things happen. Just make sure to call the town clerk tomorrow," she said. The second officer watched on from the sidewalk.

They returned to their vehicles and I pulled back onto the road. Their blue lights turned off and I signaled to get onto the highway.

School was an hour's drive from me and I cried the entire way there. I cried about the humiliation of being pulled over. I cried about my plates. I cried, knowing that I was going to have to spend a large part of Valentine's Day solving the issue (goodbye brunch, goodbye day in Boston).

And I cried because I felt like, once again, my ex took something from me.

I knew it had been a confluence of events. It was a freak accident. It was remarkably bad timing. I tried to remind myself of that. It didn't matter. All that mattered was that I was going to be late to a class with one of my favorite professors, that I had lost my beloved vanity plates, that my Valentine's Day was ruined—all because I'd let a man into my life who never had my best intentions at heart. A man who took and took and took.

And there he was, taking more.

When was it going to stop?

When was he going to stop compromising my life?

I got to campus, went into the bathroom, and splashed water on my blotchy face. When that didn't get rid of the blotchiness, I rubbed a paper towel over my cheeks to get everything to flush. I

46

looked better than I had on the drive, but anyone with even a modicum of emotional intelligence would be able to tell that I wasn't okay.

... And I was about to walk into a class full of psychology graduate students.

Class was a test for staying present. I wrote extremely detailed notes. I bit my tongue or dug my nails in my arm, focusing with all my might on the physical sensation. Anything—anything—to keep my mind from wandering. Because if I thought about it, I was going to start crying again.

Just thinking about how I was trying not to think about it made me want to cry.

The most open wound was the kindness of the two officers. The kindness was a double-edged sword. Their change in demeanor had been a reflection of how rough I must've looked. Because they were responding compassionately, I had no choice but to acknowledge why I needed compassion in the first place.

Once finished, I left class as quickly as possible. I cried on my drive home. I cried as I sent voice messages to Britt, Georgia, and several other friends. I cried as I sent text messages to several more. I cried in ways that I hadn't since I'd left my last relationship. I could tell, based on how I kept telling Georgia that I knew that she'd been through worse and that I knew I was being silly, that I'd also regressed back to the person I was back in September, the timid shell of a being who felt like she had to apologize for her existence.

Valentine's Day was supposed to be the counterbalance to the fraudulent one my ex had given me the year before. But there he was, still finding ways to keep my life chaotic, like a poltergeist knocking over books and breaking priceless vases.

THE YEAR OF DATING MYSELF

Right before I fell asleep, I stumbled upon an idea. It wasn't a solution, but it was a way of reframing the experience.

It was the Year of Dating *Myself*. The year where I was my *own partner*. What would I do if I had a partner who'd gone through what I'd gone through? What if that partner came up to me, completely distraught, telling me that they'd been pulled over by the police, that they were devastated over the loss and triggered from the event. How would I respond if that partner, choked up with sorrow, lamented that it was going to ruin all the wonderful plans I'd made for us?

I'd tell them, "It's going to be okay. We're going to fix it—together."

I'd reassure them that plans were not completely ruined. The town clerk didn't open until 10 a.m., so I'd make us breakfast instead of going to brunch—and there would still be time to enjoy Boston.

I'd hold space for that sorrow, and say, "I'm so sorry you're going through this. I'm going to do whatever I can to help."

One might see that reframing as an act of dissociation. All I knew was that it helped calm something in me. It felt like I'd rescued myself from drowning, and it didn't really matter if I had to have an out-of-body experience to get to the lifeboat.

I called the town clerk the next day. The solution was mercifully simple. I looked up alternatives to my old sets of plates and found one that—while not as good as my original—was a decent second place. Before the town clerk opened, I made myself breakfast. I cried in the kitchen and gave myself all the time I needed with the tears. Once the town clerk opened, I went in, got my temporary plates, and paid for my registration renewal. They never asked me to pass in my old plates. There was something so simple yet overwhelming in that. The plates were no longer registered to my car, but they were still mine, in a sense. I went home, changed my plates, and got ready. I was exhausted, but I was going to be okay.

For Valentine's Day, I decided not to repeat my usual habits when I visited Boston and instead followed recommendations from Lindsey, partly because I could trust their taste, and partly because it would keep me out of my comfort zone. I took myself to an early dinner at the Boston Public Library, eating in the palatial indoor garden. A lady at the café complimented my outfit—which, admittedly, was a chaotic mashup. White skirt with black, knee-high boots, a trench coat over my denim Solo Tour jacket. But it gave me a little reassurance, like a cheerleader who didn't necessarily know what she was cheering on.

I strolled through Copley Square and down Boylston Street. I wandered the Public Garden at the golden hour, as the winter sun began to lean its light against the buildings. I eventually sat down by the historic cemetery in the Boston Common and spent the waning moments of sunset in heavy contemplation.

Sometimes you accidentally hit poetic parallels. The last time I was in Boston was on my birthday—and I wasn't enjoying the city so much as I was frantically dashing around, scrambling like a person picking up the contents of their purse after the seams burst. I was in Boston alone, for my birthday. I might've spent the entire day alone, had a close friend not insisted that I come over. She made me a birthday dinner and loaned a listening ear as I talked about everything that had been happening with my then-boyfriend.

I told her about the mind games, the volatility, and how it'd been escalating. I told her about my original plans for my birthday, how I'd taken upon myself to devote the entire weekend to "saving" our relationship. I told her about his convoluted stunts

THE YEAR OF DATING MYSELF

to get out of seeing me on my birthday, and how angry he got when I cried about it. I told her all of it, and she listened without asking the one question that others already had:

"*Why* are you *still* with him?"

It was poetic, in a way, how things unfolded just before Valentine's Day. It reminded me with unflinching precision just how bad things had been when I was still with him. I was back in Boston, just like I'd been in September. But instead of that frantic, hysterical haze, I was in a new, fierce iteration of myself.

Life is poetry—if you can handle a little free verse.

As night fell, I went to the bar that Lindsey had recommended. It was a swanky establishment in the heart of Downtown Crossing, a gorgeous hybrid of a library and a speakeasy. The lobby for the bar was crowded. The busyness pinged at my social anxiety. A part of me was already finding reasons to back out. But I knew that growth was waiting for me, just outside of my comfort zone. I went inside and asked if there were any spots free at the bar.

I sat in the dimly lit atmosphere, taking in the sounds, sights, and activity. The bartender was learning a new drink menu on the fly, referencing his notes as he made drink after drink. The maître d' walked around and gave every woman a white, long-stemmed rose. I gently held mine to my nose and took in the scent.

Well, look at that: flowers on Valentine's Day.

I paid my tab, and wrote, "You're doing great with the new menu! Happy Valentine's Day!" on the receipt for the bartender and made my way to the theater.

I spent the first act wearing a perpetual smile, beaming from ear to ear, immersed in the theatrical experience. My eyes darted around the set, desperate to take it all in, before realizing how much more I could absorb if I'd just let my gaze relax.

There's poetry in everything, including subtext.

I left the musical feeling euphoric, opting to walk through the historic parts of Boston in lieu of going to the nearest subway stop. I sang songs about historical plots as I walked by the building where they planned the Boston Tea Party. I traipsed past Faneuil Hall Marketplace and the oldest operating pub in America, one that had been pouring out ale while George Washington was president.

"What about Boston?!" I shouted and laughed with giddiness. I remembered the original version of one song, where Hamilton talks about Abigail Adams and says she's the boss back in Boston. Abigail Adams. My namesake. The *boss* in Boston. I took a moment to bask in the unbridled love I still had for the city. I'd long since moved away, exchanging busy streets for rural mountainsides, but I still loved it fiercely.

I still had the ability to love fiercely.

The Haymarket station greeted me like an old friend. I took the T train out to where I'd parked my car, its temporary plates prominently displayed. I drove home blasting the *Hamilton* soundtrack. I relished almost every song, but deliberately skipped one: the song of a young, naïve woman, celebrating how helpless she is in the face of love, a lightness to her voice as if she wouldn't be burning letters in the second act, condemning her unfaithful, self-interested husband, watching all her delicate, helpless love shatter into ashes.

Chapter 8: Ice-Skating

Some of my date plans focused on returning to the activities that had fallen by the wayside.

Once upon a time, I ice-skated regularly. Gabe, the man I went on to marry right out of college, played hockey and introduced me to the world of ice-skating. It was an innocent, if not heartbreaking tableau: a nineteen-year-old field mouse in human form, judging herself before she even stepped on the ice, and her then-boyfriend, a brilliant college boy, encouraging her to keep trying.

Going to the ice rink ran a similar path to our marriage: it quietly went off course, unnoticed until too late. There was foolhardy reassurance that it could get back on track, but a key ingredient was missing, and, eventually, it was undeniable that it was over. My hockey skates had gathered dust in the basement. I cleaned them off and returned to the rink for the first time in a decade.

The changing rooms greeted me with a pungent, yet familiar, odor as I walked past: the smell of hockey player sweat. It immediately brought me back to the ice rinks in Boston. I laced up my skates and eyed the ice. For a Thursday afternoon, it was surprisingly busy. People skated around the rink while a few figure skaters practiced in the center.

I had no idea how I'd fare, but I wasn't going to let that shake me. I took myself ice-skating, after all. The only person I had to encourage me was *me*. I tentatively stepped out on the ice and was surprised at how natural it felt. I did a few laps around the rink before I attempted some of the basics. I tried my forward crossovers, crossing one foot over the other to turn. I practiced skating backwards. I practiced my hockey stops—a maneuver I'd never mastered, and it was clear the shakiness was still there. But I found myself spellbound to the ice for the next hour, even as the chill in the air settled into my bones.

I could never do something like that when I was younger: I was too anxious to stay on the ice for that long. I remembered the countless free skates I attended, where I kept my mind occupied by constantly counting down the minutes.

There was no present moment for younger me—just a constant anticipation of the future.

But I still remembered those times fondly. I remembered how Gabe stepped into his element on the ice. I remembered the joy in realizing I could skate backwards. I remembered how ravenous I was by the end of free skate, devouring our lunch at the local pizzeria. There was so much happiness in those moments. It was easy to think of my twenties as a time of hardship and mistakes. But there had been so much good in them too.

As the public skate neared its end, I made my way off the ice and packed away my skates. I stood up and attempted to get acclimated to the solid ground again. I drove home exhausted, but happy. It was a triumphant return, and I promised myself to make it a regular outing.

I made good on my promise and got back on the ice a few weeks later. My transition from skating forward to skating backward was getting smoother. My forward crossovers felt more natural. But the second outing shined light on an unexpected area, and an old memory soon consumed me. I'd resigned myself to the inevitable reunion to all the pain that I'd been running from, but I wasn't expecting it to hit like it'd been sprinting to catch up.

The memory was from when I was twenty years old. I was watching Gabe play hockey. Only, I wasn't *really* watching. I had both earbuds in, blaring music from my iPod and playing solitaire. I didn't know it until after the game, but—*twice*—Gabe had scored a goal. *Twice*, he'd skated over to where I was in the bleachers, to celebrate with me. *Twice*, I was lost in my own world and didn't hear him, even when he tapped on the glass to get my attention.

"You don't have to come to my hockey games anymore," he said afterward.

"But I want to!" I protested.

"Let me restate: I don't want you at my hockey games anymore."

I felt terrible then, but it was nothing compared to the onslaught I felt, seventeen years later.

Seventeen years had only helped all that evaded pain gain momentum.

I'd always had a profound disconnect between my logic and my emotions. Both sides were outstandingly strong, and yet with a chasm between them, so logic could never share ground with my emotions. It didn't matter that I knew that I was young. It didn't matter that I wouldn't be diagnosed with attention-deficit/hyperactivity disorder for another seven years. It didn't matter that I was a decade out from realizing just how pathologically self-involved my unexamined trauma had made me. All I could do was picture that man in his early twenties, skating over with excited eyes to celebrate his goals with his girlfriend, only to have that light dim when he realized she couldn't be more disinterested.

Those were the moments when no logic would get a foothold. I was convinced that I, and I alone, was the reason the marriage didn't work. That I was nothing short of a monster for it. There was irony in recently being reminded of the man who'd broken my heart because his feet pointed in the direction of his ex-wife, only for me to break my own heart as my feet pointed in the direction of my ex-husband.

But I had no time for irony, at that moment.

Sometimes I can't handle life's free verse.

I had a feeling something was up when my doctor didn't get back to me when he said he would.

"I have some bad news about the labs for genetic testing," he eventually said. "There's been a few hurdles, and it's looking like, if they'd be able to work with us, we're looking at a minimum of $2,000."

I sighed. The price tag did more than take the wind out of my sails. It stopped the boat entirely.

"There's a genetic counseling service at the hospital. I can send a referral in," he offered, and I accepted.

My quest to get tested for early onset Alzheimer's was clearly not going to be quick, direct, or simple. I had no idea exactly what I was supposed to do next. *Was I supposed to call the hospital, or would they call me?* I hoped it wasn't the former. With the wind out of my sails, I began to doubt venturing out to sea in the first place.

Somewhere in all of that, I learned that my most recent ex was copying me. He was telling his viewers that he was devoting a "Year to Dating Himself"—and that he was on a "Solo Tour." He was copying my dates, right down to the verbiage to describe them.

Stella gave me the heads up. Stella had her own axe to grind with her former friend—and found catharsis in keeping an eye out for me. I thought about how it once took monumental effort to avoid checking his social media platforms. In those first months after I left him, I was consumed with what he was saying about me. But I eventually shifted. I went from convincing myself not to check, to forgetting to check.

Only then, I was in a place where, had Stella not alerted me, I probably would've never known. The version of myself who couldn't stop checking his social media platforms would've been furious that he was copying me.

But then? I just shrugged my shoulders and smiled.

Keep watching me. Keep copying me.

I'll keep thriving.

Part III: March

Chapter 9: Corrective Experiences

I was driving to school when I got a call from the hospital.

"We received your doctor's referral, and we'd love to set up an appointment with one of our genetic counselors," said a young lady.

"Yes, that would be great!"

"All right, so, our first available appointment is July 10—"

"Sure, yeah . . . let's do that one," I said, with a twinge of disappointment. I forced myself to add: "Just to confirm, that's the *earliest*, you said?"

"Yes, that'll be the earliest anyone would be able to see you. But I can put you on a waitlist in case something opens up sooner."

"Yes, that would be great," I replied. "And that won't get rid of my July appointment, right?"

"Right. If nothing opens up, we'll just see you in July."

"Great, thank you so much."

"Of course. Have a great day."

One step closer. I was disheartened by the July date, but it was still something. There was another stone laid out on my path. I had no idea where it was leading to, but at least I wasn't standing still anymore.

A few days later, spring won a temporary victory. The edges of the brisk winter air had softened, and I took a walk around a nearby city.

Like many towns in New England, the city had been battling against decay since its mill yard days. Beautifully repurposed redbrick buildings stood next to remnants from another tent city raid. Three empty storefronts served as the opening act for a bright and sparkling chain restaurant. One side street hosted swanky restaurants, a paint bar, a palatial theater; the next street was effectively abandoned, a dystopian tableau. I made my way down the first side street, passing the swanky restaurants and the paint bar before pausing at the theater. I stood where they'd taped up flyers for upcoming events. *The Phantom of the Opera* was set to run in April.

The Phantom of the Opera was the first musical I ever fell in love with.

It was also entangled to the point of knotting with my ex.

The musical had been used as the keystone for some of his more insidious acts. When we first began dating, he had recounted the heart-wrenching tale of his beloved girlfriend—a woman he met while doing a production of *Phantom*—and how, one night, they got into a fight and he stormed out of her apartment, only for him to learn later that evening that she had passed away. It was a tale that tore at my sympathies—and once he realized that it would be a topic that I'd always back down on, he weaponized it every chance he got.

He'd invoked her name constantly; her ghost became his most powerful tool for control. He'd parade photos of them sharing the stage during their production of *Phantom*. He did this sometimes to deflect (how dare I question the actions of a grieving man?), but sometimes it was to just be cruel, to remind me of my place.

My stomach turned upon hearing or seeing anything in relation to the musical, after that. My beloved musical had been weaponized against me, and I was tired of equating it to the barrel of a gun.

I went in and bought a ticket.

I didn't want my entire self-dating journey to be a reaction to my last relationship, but I also didn't want to deny the avenues that needed healing. It was akin to how I once bought coffee from a local café until it stopped feeling like a time capsule for a first date with an old boyfriend, years ago.

Sometimes things are done to stare down the monster under the bed, if only to prove the monster was never there in the first place.

I confirmed my ticket with anticlimactic ease. Sometimes the biggest victories are where the war looks more like a deserted battleground.

But, at the same time, it didn't stop me from remembering my fury when I learned that my ex's heart-wrenching tale was a complete fabrication. She was never his girlfriend; they were barely even talking to each other when she passed away.

I learned the truth when people—specifically those from his local community—started reaching out to me. I'd already learned so many lies, but that one turned my heart to ice. I understood then that there was a place past rage, one that felt like both the eye of and the cause of the storm.

All those memories, those feelings, dredged up just from buying my ticket.

It was why I *needed* to see the show. So much was churning below the surface. I had to do whatever it took to keep myself from drowning in it.

My new license plates came in later that week.

I looked at my old plates, sitting in my drying rack after I'd washed the last seven years of grime off them. I remember how lucky I felt when I got them, amazed that such a vanity plate hadn't been snagged up yet. It still hurt to know that it wasn't mine anymore.

But as I installed my new license plates, the words slipped right out of me:

"It's just not my turn with those plates anymore."

It was a new chapter, and somehow the new plates represented that.

A few of my friends had tried to cheer me up by bashing the new owner of my original plate configuration, but I waved it away. She was not some evil person who'd been waiting for her chance to strike. She was probably someone who'd gotten a new car and felt a sentimental draw to the same word. She, too, probably couldn't have believed her luck that it was available. It was her turn with that vanity plate. Without either of us knowing it, there'd been a passing of the torch.

I was in a new era. The bright and shiny new plates—plates that hadn't yet dealt with harsh weather and road conditions—were my signal of it.

"The crows!!" I shouted from my car.

I looked up during my drive home from my rock-climbing gym and saw at least twenty crows hanging out in the trees. A convenience store sat at a nearby corner and I immediately pulled in.

When I'd written *Befriend a murder of crows* on my list, I assumed it was more of a fanciful dream than an accomplishable goal. I'd never expected anything to come from it. I grabbed a container of peanuts at the convenience store, paid the cashier, and walked back out. I poured out some of the peanuts and followed the steps I'd been advised to take when signaling your intentions to the crows. None of the crows came down, but I'd been warned that it can be a slow process. It takes time to build trust.

Signaling trustworthiness means nothing if there isn't consistent action to back it up.

If only I could remind the past versions of myself of that.

Chapter 10: Intimacy, Robbery, Infancy

It took until March for me to even think about sex.

Well, no. That's not entirely accurate.

I'd been thinking about it. Just not the way one would expect.

I never had an easy relationship with it. I was taught at too young an age that touch was dangerous. By the time I was an adult, my body felt like something I had to safeguard. It was only during times of safety that I'd even let that side out to breathe—and the threshold for what felt safe only got higher with each violating encounter.

At the beginning of my last relationship, my Prince Charming pretended to understand. But the attuned lovemaking was soon replaced by disinterested, selfish use. The bedroom became emblematic of the relationship: there was a pleading in my actions, a begging to be seen, to be worthy. But my frantic efforts only highlighted how blatantly I was being used. It was a pain that amplified when I learned he'd been cheating.

In the aftermath, I shut down completely.

I did my best to reframe things, the same way I reframed getting pulled over before Valentine's Day. But it still gnawed at me.

Something got taken away from me, and all the self-compassion in the world couldn't change that.

I was reminded of this robbery every time I watched a movie's love story and felt myself split in two. One side of me sneered, convinced they were all just putting on a front to make her *think* she'd found her prince. Another side of me—the side that had always been a hopeless romantic—ached.

In some ways, the ache was a good thing. The ache meant that I hadn't shut down completely. The ache meant that I felt safe enough to *want*. But the ache also solidified my cynicism. That ache had previously served as the dinner bell for every bad player. That ache had been the siren call as I crashed my ship upon the rocks.

I hated the state I was in. Yes, I was nurturing a sense of safety in my own company. But I'd also been robbed of the part of me that thought she could lay her heart down at the feet of a man and trust that he wouldn't stomp on it.

But there was also no denying that I was touch starved.

Despite learning that touch was dangerous, I had an insatiable need for it. Even a hand hold or a graze of the neck. Platonic cuddling wasn't an option: most of my friendships were long-distance, and I was still trying to teach my body that most friends aren't waiting for their moment to take advantage of you. I knew one way to mitigate the starvation was through massages, but it was like getting a few slices of bread when you're desperate for a meal.

I tried reminding myself that I'd been navigating my starvation for a while. My last relationship was long-distance—and, despite seeing each other only sporadically, he had made me feel like requesting a hug or kiss was akin to asking for the moon and stars.

But there's triage in emotional pain, and sometimes that can act as protection. I was consumed with misery in my last relationship.

When you're too busy begging your boyfriend to treat you with respect, to actually love you, you're less likely to realize how long it's been since someone held your hand.

By mid-March, I had organized all my childhood toys.

I took out every stuffed animal, one by one, and welcomed them home. I flipped through my childhood books, unlocking memories with each page. I cleared out space on a mantle and placed my plastic horses on them.

I eventually found a stack of baby photos.

I looked through them gingerly. I'd seen them all before, but a detail in one photo stopped me in my tracks: I was a chunky blob of an infant, in her car seat, staring at the camera with a slightly amused smile. In the car seat sat a pink stuffed bear and brown plush dog.

My heart seized.

Those very stuffed animals had just been welcomed home.

They weren't just my childhood toys—they were my *infant* toys.

I had my baby toys. These little comfort items had been by my side since the beginning.

They were home again.

When I told my friends about my visit in January, I'd noted how little it bothered me when my mom didn't recognize me at first.

"I mean, my mom hasn't recognized me as her daughter in years," I said. "The only difference is that, now, it's more literal."

Somewhere during my childhood, my mom had started seeing me more as a threat than as her daughter—and started treating me as such.

But I replayed in my head that moment when she stared at me blankly before lighting up about "her" Abby. She looked at me the way one looks at a stranger, but her face brightened at remembering *her daughter.*

THE YEAR OF DATING MYSELF

Once upon a time, she was a loving mother. She'd just been progressively losing her ability to see me as "her" Abby.

But, deep down, past the decaying gray matter in her brain, there was a "her" Abby that she loved dearly.

That knowledge both shattered me and put me back together.

Chapter 11: Solo, and Dueling

I woke up before the sunrise, one late March morning.

I got out of bed and looked outside. The sky was a royal blue, tinged with light at the horizon. It was a clear morning, with barely a cloud in the sky. The perfect kind of morning to take myself out on a sunrise coffee date. I swung by my town's coffee shop and started driving to a nearby lake. The park by the lake faced directly east and I arrived right as the pink hues of morning adorned the treetops. I got out of my car and sat on a nearby bench. The air was frigid and the lake was half frozen, giving everything an ethereal feel. The sun bounced off the ice in diffused light as it came up.

I saw two crows in the tree by the bench. I returned to my car, grabbed my jar of peanuts, and stepped back out, calling for them in a series of whistles. I scattered a few nuts on the bench, looked at them, looked at the peanuts, looked at them again, and went back to my car. They were still in the tree when I left, but that was to be expected.

Humans are cruel creatures, at the end of the day. Some even take the time to earn trust before they carry out their misdeeds. The crows had every right to keep their distance.

There's a reason why the dodo bird went extinct. Blind trust is an evolutionary dead end, in the wrong hands.

The memory of Gabe's hockey game was still on my mind weeks later.

I wanted to talk to him about it, but I was cautious about saying anything. It was common during our marriage for me to hand my emotions over to him, effectively saying, "here, you fix it." I didn't want to unload my sadness at the cost of his emotional labor.

But a conversation toward the end of the March naturally shifted in that direction.

I did my best to control the tremble in my voice as I told him how skating had reopened the hockey memory—and that I was sorry for the pain I'd caused.

"I don't need that apology," he said. "I mean, at one point, I needed you to see the hurt that it caused me and not focus so much on how it must mean you're a bad person. But I'm glad you're doing the work."

If that had been a movie, the conversation would've been the resolution scene, perhaps with the two of us out for coffee, cradling our cups as the movie's side story arc comes to a satisfying conclusion. Instead, it was a casual conversation before the topic shifted elsewhere. It was a healthy conversation. But it wasn't going to tie up loose ends.

But that's life. Life has more loose ends than neatly tied bows— and pretending otherwise will only create a bigger knot, down the road.

My last solo date for March was a dueling pianos event at a newly renovated theater. I'd bought my ticket knowing nothing about what the show entailed—but I quickly learned that it centered on song requests. If someone didn't like a requested song, they could override it with money (and another could override the override with a larger sum of money).

I sat awkwardly through the first few songs, painfully aware of my solo status. But all it took were a few irresistible beats for me to join in with the rest of the audience.

The Solo Tour was about leaning into the discomfort of having no one but myself to reinforce my experience. Previously, I'd filtered my life through my partner. Their reaction to my experience mattered more than my authentic experience. This would amplify things if they were having a good time. But if my partner were in a bad mood, all that mattered was tending to them. But there was no one to tend to at that moment—no one but me—and all I wanted to do was sing catchy songs and enjoy the evening.

I left with a gigantic smile on my face and headed back to my car. I initially planned on grabbing a drink after the show, but I was tired—and what's the point of date plans if they're done without consideration for your partner's energy levels?

I ended March with Lana's bachelorette party—and a reminder of how important communal healing is.

I'd known Lana since our college years in Boston, but we became platonic life mate levels of close after she also moved to the same rural part of New England. She'd been by my side through the end of my marriage and through every dating disaster. She was one of the friends who had rallied when my then-boyfriend had upended my birthday. I was forever indebted to her kindness and support over the years.

Part of Lana's bachelorette party included a rage room: a place designed for smashing objects to smithereens. It had been on my

THE YEAR OF DATING MYSELF

list of date ideas, so it felt like kismet to go to one with Lana and her friends. Plus—after what had transpired in the days before the bachelorette party—it was going to be a needed release.

One of the people who had reached out to me after I'd left my last relationship was Danielle, a whip-smart content creator from the same social media platform I'd met my then-boyfriend on. She'd recently dealt with a similar abuser, and we bonded as we compared notes on our experiences. Then—days before Lana's bachelorette party—Danielle's abuser was publicly brought to task. A woman had come forward, which caused an avalanche of other victims to step forward, as well. It was validating to watch a carbon copy of my ex get called out, but it was also incredibly triggering.

It also reminded me that I never saw any justice for my situation.

It was no wonder that I went into the rage room brimming with pent up energy.

The rage room, on its own, was a needed release. There are few words to describe what unlocks in you when you've been given permission to destroy. But it was in what happened next that cemented itself in my memory.

"Let's take turns picking something that we want to release anger about," one friend suggested.

It was undeniable what I was going to pick.

"Fuck you, 'ex'!" I yelled when it was my turn, screaming out his name. I raised a glass vase over my head and slammed it to the ground. It shattered into a thousand pieces.

"Fuck you, 'ex'!" Lana parroted, repeating my words, smashing a teacup with a frying pan.

"Fuck you, 'ex'!" repeated another woman in the party, who threw a plate into a wall.

I watched these women—half of whom didn't even know me, let alone my ex—shout my words with the same level of conviction.

A deep fissure of pain started to heal.

This is why our ancestors had ceremonies, I thought. While Lana had been the only one in the group to bear witness to my suffering, all of them were bearing witness to my healing.

Before the rage room—and in the immediate aftermath of the whistleblowing—Danielle had said to me: "In some ways, I was lucky. All of us women? We had each other. We had a sisterhood. You had to navigate your situation alone, and that wasn't fair."

Her words echoed in me as we left the rage room.

I might not have had a legion of fellow victims who were willing to speak publicly. But I wasn't alone. I had people who had stuck their necks out to validate my experience. I had friends who'd stepped up when everything fell apart. I was surrounded by people who were ready to pledge some of their destruction in the name of my rebuilding.

Maybe what happened to me wasn't fair. But I wasn't alone.

I had my sisterhood with me.

Part IV: April

Chapter 12: Thunder and Lightning

A thunderstorm greeted the first day of April.

I stepped out onto my porch and watched the light show in the distance. The rain hadn't arrived yet, but it was clear from the constant lightning that it was going to be intense. I went inside, grabbed my fuzzy blanket, and sat on my porch bench.

The thunder shifted from a constant rumble to intermittent, loud cracks. The rain started coming in waves, obliterating the view past my lawn. The lightning was so vibrant that it brightened the world around me. I watched on, safe, warm, and dry. I cuddled into my blanket, murmuring: "I'm counting this as a solo date."

Like any romantic relationship, the small moments mattered just as much—if not more—than the big ones. Life exists in the day-to-day. Love flourishes in the times when there's nothing more than the genuine presence of each other.

April was gearing up to be the busiest month. I was in the final lap of my spring semester. I was set to fly out to Vegas, reuniting with Britt for an award show ceremony. Lana's wedding followed. I had my concert at the beginning of the month and *Phantom of the Opera* at the end of it. But, at that moment, I was sitting still, watching the storm come in—witnessing the show around me, knowing that I was safe where I was. Simultaneously at ease and in the middle of things.

The concert I'd bought a ticket for on New Year's Eve had finally arrived. The day marked something for me that words couldn't properly describe. When I'd purchased that ticket, the Year of Dating Myself was barely a spark of an idea. I'd gone into the new year with a scattered list, determination, and little else.

But there I was, four months later.

I drove to the concert, blasting all my favorite songs. I went into the venue and found my seat. I sat down, the only one in the row. I thought little of it at first. The show was sold out, after all, and I'd arrived early. Eventually, two people sat in the seats by the aisle on one side. During the opening act, three sat in the seats on the other aisle. Then there was me: in a middle seat, with two empty seats on either side of me.

Self-consciousness kicked in. I was hidden at the dueling pianos event, surrounded by people. But at the concert, I felt like the outcast child in the lunchroom, whose isolation was highlighted by the empty seats surrounding them. I took a breath and reminded myself that the goal wasn't to hide that I was by myself, but to revel in it.

Yes, I'm here, solo. I'm here because my company can be enough. Is that a problem?

The anxiety slipped away as my favorite band came on. I danced to the fast-paced songs. I held my hands to my heart at the ballads. I sang lyrics at the top of my lungs. By the end, I'd hoped that the people behind me not only saw that I was alone but found my solo antics amusing. I walked out with a smile on my face and my ears ringing. As I cut across the sidewalk to get to my car, I heard two people talking behind me.

"No, those women were obnoxious," said one of them. "They were shouting every single lyric and it's like, okay, cool, you know all their songs . . ."

I froze. I thought about all the songs I sang at the top of my lungs. Were they talking about me?

I replayed what they had said and smirked. While, yes, it was my reminder to be more considerate of other concert goers, they weren't talking about me. They were complaining about *multiple* women being obnoxious.

And I was—decidedly—*alone*, after all.

A few days later, I had a spa facial.

Touch starvation was still an issue. I knew how badly it could affect me. I felt lost after my marriage ended—literally and physically, like my body had been set adrift at sea. The facial was necessary. I needed someone touching my face, even if it was just to apply the cleanser. I needed someone stroking my neck, even if it was just the massage as the mask set.

Two thoughts came to mind on my drive home after.

The first was a memory: the boyfriend who repeatedly left me for his ex-wife had loved getting his head scratched. I wasted no opportunity to give him what he loved. After a while, I mustered the courage to tell him that I liked my hair played with too. I showed him how to do it—even demonstrated the reaction he'd get from me. After doing all that work to show him what I loved, he casually remarked, "ah, good to know. Just, y'know, remind me. Because I'm sure I'm going to forget."

My heart sank. He'd already decided that that information wasn't for safekeeping. He'd been given a veritable workshop on how to make his girlfriend feel cherished—and he was already making her responsible for reminding him to make her feel that way.

I never had to be reminded that he loved head scratches.

My second thought was a realization: while I became dizzy with touch starvation after my marriage ended, dating never sated my hunger. It was far more than my last relationship being long distance. The men I dated never really touched or held me, unless it was to engage in sex. I tried to work around my starvation by doting on *them*. I attempted to get my needs met by frantically meeting *theirs*.

It was a bittersweet realization. On the one hand, dating myself wouldn't mean a drop in affectionate touch. But on the other hand, it meant I'd been as good as alone for years, with men I'd wasted my affection on.

I'd given them a feast, and they'd left me to starve.

I wasn't completely out of the woods with my license plates. A set of bills from the highway toll company let me know that I'd never updated my plates with them. I went into the toll pass's office the day before my Vegas trip. I walked up to the next available teller and explained my situation.

"Oh, this is an easy fix," said the teller. "Let's change the plate on file."

The teller typed away before pausing.

"Hmm, we've hit a snag."

"A snag?"

"It seems you're not on the account."

I let out a sigh. I still shared the account with Gabe, one of the minutiae that we saw no need in separating. I wasn't surprised that my name wasn't on the account. When we were married, I'd let Gabe take care of everything, and usually gave up having any say in the process. It was one of the many things that had contributed to the end of our marriage.

"Who's Gabe?" asked the teller.

I gave a knee-jerk answer.

"My husband."

It was the easiest answer at the moment. Did I really want to lay my personal life at the feet of a stranger?

("Oh, he's my ex-husband—but like not in a negative way! He's one of my best friends now, and we still share things like the toll pass account . . .")

But something hit me as I answered. I bit my tongue and held back. I held back as I texted Gabe, asking him to add me to the account. I held back as they updated my license plate.

I held back as I smiled, said goodbye, and went back to my car.

Which is when I let go.

And I cried.

I want to make it very clear what I was crying about. By this point, I wouldn't be surprised if some of you readers have started to wonder if I wanted to get back with Gabe—or if we *would* get back together. I know what it looks like from the outside. To the unsuspecting eye, it looks like a tale of a woman realizing, through her time being single, that she should reconcile with her college sweetie.

I'll try my best to let said readers down gently: that's never going to happen.

I wasn't crying about how my ex-husband was—well—my ex. The fact that we thrived as friends wasn't a sign that we should get back together, but that we'd made the right decision.

I was crying because there was once a version of me who believed she was meant for the white-picket-fence-two-point-five-kids life. There was simplicity for the woman who felt like she was getting rewarded for playing by the rules. The simplicity had come at the cost of authenticity. I knew that. But all I could think about was that heartbreakingly innocent twentysomething who thought

THE YEAR OF DATING MYSELF

she knew what the rest of her life would bring. A woman who could talk about "my husband," and evoke a by-the-books life. I sobbed, mourning the life I once thought I could handle, mourning a path that, at least in that moment, felt so peaceful.

I grieved the loss of innocence. I'd taken a bite of the fruit from the tree of knowledge. My eyes were open, and I was all too aware of how exposed I was. I felt like I'd been kicked out of the garden, and I had no one to blame but myself. I'd grown. I'd become wiser. I'd become the person I was meant to be. I wouldn't trade that for anything—certainly not for my old life.

The caterpillar must completely dissolve first in order to transform into the butterfly. But all I could do, during that drive back from the toll pass office, was mourn the caterpillar and romanticize a world where all you do is crawl around and eat leaves.

Chapter 13: Inner Teen

" . . . and what does that say about you?"

I was catching my therapist up on the whistleblowing of Danielle's abuser. I told my therapist about the parallels to my ex—and the fury that came with watching one abuser be held accountable while the other skirted by.

"What does that say about me?" I readjusted in my seat. "I mean, nothing. It was a matter of circumstances. The person who hurt Danielle had hurt a lot of women in a short amount of time. Many with big online platforms that they could share their story on . . ."

"Oh, how I love Logic Abby!" said my therapist. "She always has an airtight case. Really, if I didn't know any better, I'd think that was actually how you felt!"

I took in a breath.

"You know what I'm going to ask next," she added.

My shoulders dropped. Her ability to sniff out when I was intellectualizing my emotions was *why* she was my therapist. She knew all my clever hiding spots. I loved that about her.

I also kind of hated it.

"I know . . ." I responded.

THE YEAR OF DATING MYSELF

"If Emotional Abby got a chance to talk, what would she say?"

Those were the magical words that, by that point, always shattered my defenses.

The emotions swelled and my eyes welled up with tears.

"It says my abuse is not worth demanding justice for," I replied.

"You know, it's interesting," said my therapist. "For a long while, we were working with the wounded child part of you. The one who thought she didn't deserve love, or safety. And I'm not hearing that, here."

I could only nod.

"What part of you, do you think, is that feeling coming from, then?"

"I agree, I don't think it's wounded-child me . . ." I said, and then trailed off.

"When did you start speaking up about your family?"

"I'm not exactly sure," I said. "Maybe high school?"

"I think of those childhood memories we processed," said my therapist. "Inevitably, we'd run into anger and we'd hit a wall. No matter what we did, we'd always circle back to that anger."

"Once I believe that I didn't deserve it, I'm then furious about it."

"Another way to look at that, potentially," said my therapist, "is that, once the wounded child is healed enough, the inner teen comes through."

I took a slow breath. We'd spent so much time tending to the little child side of me. I'd found my way into loving that side. I'd waded through the sorrow that came once the protective layer of self-hatred was removed, and I got to really convince that side of me that she was safe.

The same way a child grows up into a teen, we'd just had a similar development.

The wounded inner child had been healed (or at least healed enough). My inner teen finally needed tending to.

Chapter 14: Lady Luck Is on My Side

The morning before my flight to Vegas did not go according to plan: that's an understatement if I ever heard one.

I had originally planned on sitting in the terminal, waiting to board, typing dutifully away at my laptop, and making headway on the papers that I had due. Instead, I sprinted across two terminals at Boston Logan International Airport, begged people to let me cut in line at the Transportation Security Administration, and got to my plane literally minutes before the gate was scheduled to close.

(When I say minutes, I mean minutes: I had my ticket scanned at 8:48. The gate was scheduled to close at 8:50.)

Everything that could've gone wrong, did: subway delays, a car crash at the airport that caused standstill traffic, and shuttle bus issues, including continuous issues with its replacement: a shuttle bus that skipped my terminal entirely, causing me to get off at the next stop and sprint across two terminals.

The people in line at the TSA graciously let me cut in front. But, in all the chaos, I'd forgotten to empty out my water bottle in my backpack, which held me up. My carry-on bag was also held up thanks to my gift for Britt. I nervously listed off everything in the box, petrified they were about to rip open the gift wrap.

THE YEAR OF DATING MYSELF

"Please, my plane is already boarding," I heard myself pleading.

I eventually got my bags back—my water bottle empty, Britt's gift mercifully untouched—only to realize that my gate was on the opposite end of the longest terminal.

The only time I wasn't on the verge of tears was when I was sprinting, with onlookers cheering me on. I got to my gate sweating, beet red, and shaking. I had to check my carry-on since I was—quite literally—the last person they checked in. But still, I made it, and there was something symbolic about the whole ordeal.

True, everything had gone wrong. But everything else had to go *right* for me to make it in time. I'd been trying to see the events in my life in the same fashion: when everything in my life went wrong, everything else had to go right for me to get to the other side of things.

After takeoff, I used the spike in adrenaline to crank out the final sections of a paper. Two hours later, with the paper finished, my adrenaline dropped and I wondered if I was going to throw up, pass out, or both. I nibbled at my in-flight snack. I fretted about items in my luggage getting broken or smashed. I thought about everything that I didn't think to take out of my carry-on before handing it over.

Like Britt's gift.

Britt was going to be a presenter at the award show ceremony. In celebration of that, I'd made Britt a type of swag bag like the ones Hollywood presenters get. I've been told that I'm a good gift giver—and I once poured that talent exclusively into my romantic relationships. I paid close attention to their interests, their hobbies, the things they wanted and the activities they enjoyed. My gifts screamed from the mountaintops: "You are seen! You are loved! You are cherished!"

My gifts also screamed, "does this finally make me worthy of love too?"

After leaving my last relationship, I took stock in the toll that gift giving had taken on me. Gifts were an extension of that imbalance in relationships. My gifts were yet one more thing they could take without reciprocating, and I'd walk away drained. In the Year of Dating Myself, I actively redirected that energy to my friends—and the difference was night and day. Instead of drained, I felt energized. Instead of used, I felt appreciated. Gift giving for my friends had been a corrective experience. A path that had originally caused me pain, brought me a happy ending.

Britt's award show gift bag (which, admittedly, was in a box, because a bag wouldn't have survived the trip) was a corrective experience on another level too. A month before I left, my last ex was slated to host the yearly ceremony for his community arts group. I threw myself into making him a swag bag, filled with gifts, trinkets, and all his favorite treats.

I never got a chance to give it to him. Days before the ceremony, he yelled at me and then used our "fight" for why I shouldn't see him that weekend. The proceeding month became one of the most confusing, stressful, and heartbreaking times of my life—and, with each week, I'd watch the bag become more tainted. When I finally broke up with him, a part of me had considered giving it to him when he'd be in town and had promised to drop off my things from his place—but the idea of giving him the bag made my stomach churn.

Dismantling the gift bag broke my heart more than leaving the relationship. It represented all my care and devotion going to waste.

My gift bag to Britt was a way to walk down that extremely specific, extremely painful path, and perhaps finally see a happy ending. It only heightened my worry about my carry-on bag, a worry that heightened as I touched down in Vegas and one of the trams to the luggage carousels was out of order. The platform for the one working tram became suffocatingly crowded. It took three rounds before I finally got onto a tram.

"I'm between carousels eight and ten!" Britt texted as I got off the tram.

"I'm so lost," I replied. I began to type what landmarks were around me when I heard my name shouted out in a wonderfully familiar voice.

I turned around to see Britt standing there, holding a small whiteboard sign like a car service chauffeur. Only the whiteboard read:

"Turdsicle."

I put down my backpack, gave Britt a hug, and burst into tears.

"These are good tears! I promise they're good tears!" I kept saying.

And they were. After all the stress of the morning, after teetering on the edge of breakdown, there we were. The agonies of our obstacles fade into the background in light of what makes them worthwhile. We walked to my baggage carousel. My walk turned into a jog once I saw my bag. I grabbed it, surreptitiously checked inside, and breathed a sigh of relief when I saw the box intact, its wrapping paper still relatively pristine.

"I can't believe we're here!" said Britt as we took a taxi to the hotel.

"It still doesn't feel real."

I could barely contain myself once we got to our hotel room. There was so much to do, but all I wanted to do was give her the gift. I gave up finding a decent segue and simply pulled the box from my carry-on, awkwardly holding it and telling her that it was her award show gift bag (in a box).

I watched her face relax as she saw it. I started rambling about the gift (a ramble that only worsened as it dawned on me that she might think I'd only made her the gift because of my ex). She opened the box, cherishing each item in it. She pulled out the trophy I got her and put the rest of the box down.

"'*Best Turdsicle Ever,*'" Britt read the base of the trophy. "Abby!"

"Turdsicle"—our term of affection—had been mutually used for the other, for this trip.

It's a crime, how we're taught that deep, profound, nourishing love can only come from romantic bonds, that platonic love cannot carry the bells and whistles that make our souls sing.

The first events weren't until the evening. I asked Britt if she'd be interested in joining me as I rode the giant Ferris wheel that accented the Vegas skyline (the answer to *Where can I find a giant Ferris wheel?* on my Solo Tour list) and she was immediately on board.

The High Roller wasn't like a carnival Ferris wheel. It was a constant, slow-moving machine, where riders hop on and off as the carriage traverses the platform. We got a carriage to ourselves and leaned into our silliness as we made our way to the top. We watched a Bellagio fountain show. We gazed at the mountains. We took pictures of each other, taking pictures of the other.

Someone once asked me if I'd count something as a stop on my Solo Tour if a friend had been part of it. I'd told them, "Without a doubt, yes."

Perhaps that meant it wasn't strictly a *solo* tour—but how much of a disservice we do to ourselves, believing we must pull our emotional baggage by our bootstraps, all by ourselves. Platonic community is where we can build ourselves up, especially when the romantic world has torn us down. I was learning to celebrate the story of my life, outside of romantic fairy tales. And I really began to prefer those stories.

The award show was an offshoot of a charity organization. It was also another corrective experience. I was supposed to go to the

THE YEAR OF DATING MYSELF

previous year's ceremony, back when my last ex was my new boy-friend. He talked up his role in the show and how I'd be his arm candy. But then he called me at the last minute with an uncanny story of how the charity had just betrayed him—and he wasn't going. After I left him, I'd learned that he'd asked no fewer than two other women to be his plus one for that award show.

But there I was, one year later, at that very same show.

When everything has gone wrong, everything else has to go right.

Those were the moments that convinced me of a higher power running the show. What were the odds that one of my best friends would be a presenter—and that she'd want me as her plus one? The universe loves its parallels when their writing redemption arcs.

Britt's brother, Ryan, joined us for the weekend. We got to spend Saturday afternoon feeling like VIPs in our private cabana at the pool party—and we spent Saturday night dressed up in black and gold for the dance party. In between those events, Britt went to a meeting for the presenters. She'd also gotten a chance to talk with the woman in charge of the award show—the same woman who'd overseen the previous year's show. Without me even asking, Britt had decided she'd get to the bottom of what really happened. Some-times friends aren't just the ones who'd help you bury a body; they're the ones who'll help you uncover the truth.

"Oh. My. God." Britt's face lit up when she returned from the meeting. "The only truth was that he'd been asked to be a pre-senter, which he turned down when he found out he wouldn't be paid. That's it. Everything else was fabricated."

When sifting through the rubble of emotional aftermath, hav-ing the truth is like enlisting the help of a crane operator. Suddenly the debris isn't so insurmountable. The truth is like being exoner-ated for a crime you didn't commit and watching the perpetrator be led off in handcuffs.

The scales of justice feel a little more balanced.

The weekend was a chance to be fun and free. It was on that weekend that I realized Las Vegas isn't necessarily about gambling or getting wasted—it's about having permission to be as "extra" as you want to be. There's no worry about toning yourself down. You can step into your braveness, even if that braveness just looks like a pair of platform shoes and a glittery eyeshadow.

I borrowed Britt's bravery as I started telling strangers how much I loved their outfits. Britt borrowed some of my bravery as she prepared for her role as presenter on Sunday night. Then, we ate like royalty after the show.

Soon after dinner, however, I had to catch a taxi to the airport. I had a red-eye flight. There'd been no Monday morning flights to Boston, and I wasn't going to miss my Monday evening class. I finalized packing as Britt dropped something off for a fellow presenter. Ryan stayed in the room, quietly typing up something for work.

"I'm really glad I got to meet you this weekend," I said, in my final minutes before leaving. Ryan had a lot of Britt's essence about him. It was no wonder we'd hit it off.

"Me too," he said. He got up from his seat and gave me a final hug goodbye, adding: "Britt is really lucky to have someone like you."

I closed my eyes and hugged a little tighter.

"I'm lucky to have someone like her," I replied, my heart full and breaking at the same time. I nervously texted Britt, wondering where she was. I walked into the elevator lobby, only to see her coming out of one of the elevators.

"Perfect timing!" I exclaimed, and she rode with me back down to the first floor.

"Text me when you land," she said as she hugged me, and the taxi driver asked if both of us were going.

THE YEAR OF DATING MYSELF

I navigated through the airport, the experience markedly calmer than my flight in. I took one of the trams—the trams all operational again—to my gate and struggled to keep my eyes open long enough to get on board.

I slept the kind of deep sleep where I'd close my eyes with what felt like a blink, check the time, and realize three hours had passed. Red-eye flights have a different kind of energy. The flight attendants feel like nursery attendants, there to make sure their children are tucked in and provide snacks for those who can't sleep. In between my naps, I peered out the window and watched the sun slowly make its way above the clouds.

As morning drew closer, I searched on my phone for plane tickets to Missouri. Georgia, the friend who'd invited me to her New Year's Eve trip, was going to be a host for the St. Louis Pride weekend in June—and I told her that it was the perfect excuse to come out and see her.

It wasn't easy, seeing the airline prices. I'd finished the Vegas trip knowing I was going to have to dip into savings to pay my credit card bill. It was the first time I had to contend with the idea that my Year of Dating Myself was potentially operating outside of my budget.

But life is short. The plane tickets were undeniably going to be the biggest drain on my bank account, but, if I kept my wits up, I knew I could make it work.

We landed in Boston by 8:30 in the morning. The weather was cold and rainy. I stayed awake just long enough to walk to my car and drive home. I crawled into bed with my airport clothes on and slept for four hours straight. The weather was terrible and my brain was groggy and it took everything in me not to just skip class after all (after all that teacher's pet, perfect attendance fussing). But I forced myself out of bed, into the shower, and eventually onto the road.

I listened to the voice messages waiting for me from Britt as I made the hour trek up to campus. Some of the messages filled my heart so much I could barely stand it. She thanked me for being there for her—like she hadn't been there, for me, through the absolute worst. She talked about her own flight, which took off that morning.

She also talked about Missouri, and flying out in June as well.

Long distance friendships come with a heavy cost. While compatibility knows no geography, our day-to-day lives are all too aware of it. It's hard when time together comes at a literal price, to the tune of hundreds of dollars.

But what's an extra credit card payment when you've finally found your people?

Life is short, after all.

Chapter 15: The Theater

There I was, a grown woman, having just learned how common it was for venues to sell lone remaining seats at discount prices. I'd gotten my ticket to *Hamilton* for half price—but it wasn't until I saw an ad for my favorite comedian and clicked on the nearly sold-out event that I realized it hadn't been an anomaly.

Aside from a scattering of mezzanine seats, there was one lonely spot in the box seats, stage right. It was the third wheel of the row—the other two already claimed for—and sold for cheaper than seats in the mezzanine. I'd just paid off my credit card bill for Vegas, and the sticker shock still lingered. But how was I going to pass up seeing my favorite comedian, and for such a price?

As much as I worried about the financial sustainability of my Solo Tour, I also worried about running out of interest, ideas, and events. I didn't want it to just be something that kept me distracted before inevitably fizzling out. The box seat was very much outside of my comfort zone. The third wheel seat would highlight my solo status even more than the empty row at the concert.

Maybe the version of me from the beginning of the Solo Tour would've been too weirded out by that. She might've even paid

THE YEAR OF DATING MYSELF

extra for a seat that was farther away. But I'd made strides in those four short months, and I was ready for it.

"It's like a birthday treat," said Gabe when I told him about the ticket.

"Technically it's a few weeks before my birthday, but, basically."

"Heaven knows you'll be a better date for your birthday this year, than last year's."

"*That's* a low bar to clear."

When I first made my Solo Tour list, I had two plans that took top priority: a great Valentine's Day, and a big birthday bash.

I'd spent my previous birthday miserable and confused, heartbroken and angry. The only reason "alone" wasn't among those feelings was because of my local friends who'd rallied at the last minute.

For my birthday in the Year of Dating Myself, I wanted to celebrate the longtime friends who'd done that rallying, as well as utilize that newfound community I'd been recently welcomed into online. The idea bewildered me. So many of those friends lived across the country. Who was I to ask them to travel to see me? But I had to remind myself of the kind of people I had in my life. Those were people who'd been showing up for me in those online spaces. I knew these were people who, if they were able to, would show up physically, as well.

"You keep talking about corrective experiences," I said to myself. "After an ex who did everything to get out of driving a few hours to you for your birthday, what could be more reparative than a community of friends willing to travel the same amount for you, if not more?"

I had a point. There was a reason I was dating her.

Lana's wedding was the weekend after Vegas. The last wedding I'd gone to was with my ex, when we traveled to North Carolina at the very beginning of our relationship for his middle school friend's wedding. I couldn't shake the suspicion that he originally had no intent of going to that wedding—but the wedding was the perfect excuse to shoehorn in a vacation early in the relationship without it looking like love bombing. It was uncharitable speculation, but I'd learned that it was in my best interest to assume the worst.

Because the worst usually was the truth.

I leaned into the parallels, even wearing the same dress that I wore to the North Carolina wedding. It was a gorgeous halter dress. It deserved new memories, better memories.

It deserved to go down a similar path and get a happy ending.

I arrived early to help with setting up decorations. Everyone went to a local pub afterwards, biding time before the ceremony. It gave me a chance to talk with friends I hadn't seen in years. My friend Diane finally got to introduce me to her husband.

After the ceremony—after the dinner portion of the reception had finished and the lights had dimmed and the music had turned up—I made my way across the room to Lana, who was sitting at the sweetheart table. It was potentially the first time I'd seen her sitting still since the afternoon. She was radiant in her sparkling dress and flower headband.

I sat down in the groom's seat and surveyed the area.

"How are you doing?" I asked.

"Exhausted, if I'm being honest," she said.

"Understandably so," I responded. "You did a phenomenal job, with everything."

I glanced over at the cake—a cake that she'd made herself, from scratch. She was the same woman who'd made me a cake for my birthday, the previous year. The same woman who knew me when I was a timid twenty-one-year-old, who'd borne witness to some of the most major events in my life. The woman who devoted some of her destruction in the name of my rebuilding.

"No one's dancing yet," said Lana. "Let's fix that."

Both of us stood up and shimmied our way onto the dance floor.

We spent the rest of the night dancing before the reception drew to a close and it was time to clean up. The lights flickered on and people got to work.

I watched Diane's husband immediately go over and help disassemble the *chuppah*—the canopy the couple stand under at a Jewish wedding.

"He doesn't even know anyone here, and there he goes, just helping out," said Diane with a smile.

She paused for a moment, then added: "There *are* good ones out there."

I couldn't help but sigh. I was healing. My armor was softening. There were even a few men in my life who were giving me squishy feelings—feelings that might get mistaken for a mild crush if you squinted at it just right. However, I still wasn't in a place where I could hope. Hope still felt like a set up. Hope felt like dropping down your arms right as you're punched in the jaw.

Hope felt like turning the spikes of my armor in on myself.

"Abandon all hope, ye who enter here" isn't really a warning. It's *advice*.

Is there anything more agonizing than having hope, only to watch it get dashed, over and over again?

They call it a "mercy killing" for a reason.

My last April solo date was *Phantom of the Opera*.

Just like an adult child thinking of every painful memory before visiting an abusive parent, my ex was on the forefront of my mind, leading up to the show.

"At some point, I'm going to stop this," I told myself.

I wanted to give myself a deadline: by July, I had to be completely done. No more referencing back to my ex, no more hunts for the truth, no more *corrective* experiences.

But I thought of something Stella had said to me when I kept promising that, soon enough, I'd get him out of my system: I was allowed to take as much time as I needed to heal.

Rushing the process—forcing some trite "letting go" before its time—would not heal me.

If my father's death had taught me anything, it was that expediting the process doesn't solve the issue. It simply represses it.

Don't cut corners. Give yourself time.

I walked around town. A part of me wanted to walk down to the riverfront, where I'd taken my ex before seeing a show with him at the same theater I was about to attend. Instead, I hung a left and started walking toward the theater.

I felt something unshackle in me. While I don't believe you need to forgive in order to heal, I do believe in the power of something adjacent to forgiveness: apathy.

I couldn't force the experience—and I knew the apathy wouldn't be permanent. But sometimes your version of forgiveness is just the quiet knowing that you can't be bothered. That there is nothing more to the story but you moving on.

The opposite of love isn't hate; it's ambivalence.

I found my seat and laid the theater Playbill mindlessly on my lap. It wasn't until the couple next to me opened their Playbill that I even thought to open mine.

I flipped through the pages. I got to the main cast and felt the air rush out of me.

When I had taken my then-boyfriend to that theater, the year prior, he'd opened his Playbill, pointed to a person in the cast, and exclaimed, "I know him!"

THE YEAR OF DATING MYSELF

He then relayed a heartbreaking story of a close friendship that ended out of nowhere. One of his best friends had cut off contact—and he didn't know what happened. It had tugged at my heart-strings, especially since, earlier that day, I'd learned that a friend of mine had done the exact same thing to me. He'd been there to witness my confusion and sadness. But after I ended things, I thought a lot about that story my ex gave about his former friend—and what the real story was.

And who was one of the cast members for *Phantom of the Opera?*

There was that same former friend, in the Playbill, with contact information provided and everything.

It's always in the moments when you're the most willing to move on, that the biggest pieces just fall into your lap.

If I truly were apathetic, I would've done nothing with this information. But I knew I wasn't truly apathetic. I wasn't healed yet, and it was evident in how I bristled at the character that my ex had once played in the show. I couldn't stop myself from imagining him in that role, singing those songs, pretending he was heart-heavy, kind, and deserving of all that applause.

I drafted what I wanted to say during intermission. After the show, I sent the actor my message.

Perhaps there was going to be more to the story, after all.

Part V: May

Chapter 16: Co-opt

"What time is the actor calling you?" Nina asked.

"At 4:30," I answered.

I wasn't expecting the actor to respond back. I knew how much I was stepping out of my lane, barging into someone's life with my message. I'd plead in my message to "please, please, disregard this" if I were dredging up unwanted memories.

But the actor did respond. He was happy to discuss his former friendship—and puzzled that my ex had framed the friendship in the way that he had.

"Because that's not what happened, at all," the actor had said ominously, and asked if we could talk on the phone later.

It's hard to explain the obsession with truth after being deceived by someone you loved. You fixate on uncovering every lie. You rifle through every single memory, turning over every single thing they said, feeling like a detective hell-bent on a case.

I tried my best not to let my impending phone call impede on my time with Nina. I hadn't seen her in months, and we were finally getting a chance to catch up. Nina, the woman I was honored to call my first girlfriend, the woman whose very existence tipped my precarious scales when it came to my sexuality and I had no choice but to admit I was queer. Much like with Gabe, our shift to a platonic companionship had been natural—and so we tried to get lunch whenever we could.

Yet I couldn't help but eye the time. I had no idea what kind of phone call awaited me. Anything was possible—and, given everything, I had to be prepared for the worst.

On the surface, the phone call itself was anticlimactic.

It was a tale as old as time. A friendship consisting of a shifty, unreliable friend and a devoted, constantly forgiving friend—a friend who eventually stopped putting in the effort of two people and learned how quiet the room becomes when you're not initiating every conversation.

It wasn't exactly a crime. But it took revisiting the original story that my ex had told me—particularly, the timing of him telling it— for me to connect the dots.

Had I not found out, right beforehand, that my friend had suddenly cut off contact with me, in the exact same way?

We were having a pre-show dinner when I realized my friend had cut off contact. I'd been wondering why I hadn't heard from her, only to go online and realize the reason was because she had blocked me on everything. My then-boyfriend was by my side as I sifted through the heartache. Barely an hour later, he'd opened his Playbill and told me a virtually identical story.

How did I not see it then?

He'd had a habit of co-opting my life. He'd even sold me back my very specific trauma stories as his own. After I ended things, he started pretending that *my* experiences with *him* were actually *his* experiences with *me*.

(And to top it all off, he was copying The Year of Dating Myself.)

Realizing that he'd sold my friend-breakup back to me in real time reopened a wound. I thought about the friend who'd blocked me and wondered if my ex had anything to do with it. I wanted to just let it go, but I knew I had to process it. The people who "choose not to think about it," are the same ones who don't understand why they're having emotional breakdowns over seemingly random things.

What isn't handled consciously will then be handled unconsciously.

I'd learned that you can't bury the past. It'll just dig itself back up, and return angrier than before.

Two things can be true at once: you can genuinely want to be free from the past, and you can have no choice but to stare it down until it's forced to blink.

Chapter 17: On Hammocks, On Quiet, On Empty

I rolled out my hammock, clipped it into place, and laid down.

After an eventful April, May felt like a stalled-out car.

I was exhausted. I slept for twelve hours straight, multiple days in a row.

Stella told me how she took herself to the movies, and it reminded me of all the little things I'd been glossing over. It reminded me of that first day in April, watching the storm roll in.

What if May was more about the smaller ways that I could date myself?

I thought about that as I laid in my hammock. I stared up at the sky, at the vibrant blue.

I knew how I operated. If I wasn't careful, the Year of Dating Myself would become just one more thing I went to extreme levels with in lieu of being present with myself. Focusing only on the big-ticket items rang like the emotionally unavailable, divorced dad— the one who takes the kiddos to the baseball games and amusement parks but is absent when the kids need a shoulder to cry on. I couldn't let my Solo Tour become another time I overextended to prove I'm worthy.

THE YEAR OF DATING MYSELF

I didn't need to jump through hoops to be content with my own company.

"This hammock is a solo date," I said out loud. I felt the breeze and watched the branches of the trees move. I was going to enjoy that time with myself, the same way I'd enjoy being in the arms of a partner in a hammock. Besides, when was the last time I'd had a date in a hammock? I sent myself back in time to when I was sixteen years old and briefly dated a boy at summer camp; we spent an evening cuddling in a hammock.

. . . that wasn't the last time you had a hammock date I thought to myself, as quickly as I'd conjured up my teenage memory.

Wasn't I forgetting someone? Wasn't I forgetting how I'd redownloaded the dating apps after the man with the ex-wife left me for the second time (even though I had just sworn off dating)? Wasn't I forgetting the man I matched with and decided to see where things went?

Wasn't I forgetting that one of our first dates was a campfire and a hammock?

Perhaps I had blocked out the memory because of how much of a disaster that situation quickly became. How he dumped me to reunite with his ex-girlfriend, only to beg for a second chance—and how I took him back, only for him to break my heart a second time.

When you refuse to learn your lesson, the universe will keep presenting it to you in increasingly louder ways.

I swayed in the hammock and listened to the birds chirping. I was in my own arms now, and I was going to be the kind of partner who encouraged rest, who reminded their beloved that her authentic presence would always be enough.

Chapter 18: Salem

Something happens to the moments before and after you receive life-altering news.

A sharp line is drawn. Everything leading up to that moment becomes this naïve, innocent world. A "before" time that feels so much simpler.

And—for a while after—you will have to repeatedly venture into the "before" to drag everything over to the present, more bewildering "after."

And the process is excruciating.

Every message you hadn't responded to before, but have to. Every previous obligation that must be either canceled or muddled through. As you dip into those "before" times, you're reminded of how sweet it all was by comparison and something shatters all over again.

In the "before" time, it was simply the last day of the spring semester. Class that evening was essentially the final exam, which consisted of a mock group therapy session. I was spending the day with Lana. We'd planned to do lunch and a hike together before I drove up to class.

THE YEAR OF DATING MYSELF

That's when Gabe texted me.

Salem's cancer had returned.

Salem was one of our cats—and had been since the start of our relationship. After we'd separated, we transitioned into co-parents for Salem and his siblings. We were still finding our footing as post-marriage friends when the vet first found a tumor in Salem's stomach.

I still remember that afternoon, driving to pick Salem up from our local vet so we could drive him down to an oncology hospital just outside of Boston. I spent half an hour crying in the parking lot before going inside to get him. The tests had come back with some of the worst news we could've received: large-cell gastric lymphoma. Prognosis was grim: he was given two weeks—maybe a couple months with chemo.

But Salem had proven his prognosis wrong. He'd responded to chemo in ways that surprised even the oncologist. He went into full remission—and stayed there. Each check-up visit, he got the all clear. Soon his monthly ultrasound became semimonthly, which turned into every three months.

It lulled us into a false sense of ease. He really had beaten cancer, and all of this was behind us.

But then something shifted. He'd started to become more fussy, more needy. He started throwing up, and soon whatever he threw up was tinged with blood.

Salem had an appointment with the oncology vet on the same day I was with Lana. I was convinced he'd get the all clear, yet again. I'd convinced myself that he just had an ulcer. That he'd stressed himself out, the times I wasn't around, or his dad wasn't around—and all he'd need were some kitty antacids.

He didn't have an ulcer.

The cancer had returned.

I was oddly calm as I read Gabe's message out loud to Lana. Lana stopped what she was doing and said, "I'm pouring us some shots . . ."

I stood there, surprised at my own demeanor. I was taking the news incredibly well.

Lana handed me a shot and I knocked it back.

"It's just hard, because I was thinking of all—" My voice caught. My vision blurred with tears. My lip quivered.

Oh.

There were the emotions.

I wasn't taking the news so well, after all.

Tears spilled down my face as I tried to talk about my regrets. How he should've seen the oncology vet sooner. Chemo wasn't even up for debate. He was going back on it. It was going to be expensive, but nothing compared to the cost of losing our little boy. Lana tried to talk and broke down in tears too. We poured ourselves a second shot, hugged, then cried together. We went on our hike.

I separated myself from my feelings. I knew I had to collect myself. I couldn't go to class a hysterical mess—again. I left Lana's place and forced myself to class. How badly I wanted to skip, to just drive home and wrap myself around Salem and cry.

But if there'd been anything that I'd learned while trying to get my degree, it was that, if I didn't go to class every time there was a crisis, I would've never attended class.

It was an hour and a half drive from Lana's place to school— and I cried for all of it.

I watched a crow fly across the highway and felt my hysteria rise.

Where have you guys been? I just wanted to become your friend! You disappeared on me. Why are you here now?

THE YEAR OF DATING MYSELF

I tried to stop my tears, but my mind couldn't anchor to anything else. As I exited off the highway, I rolled down the windows and let the wind hit my face.

I stared straight ahead. Yet again I separated myself from my thoughts. I got to campus, splashed water on my face, and walked into class.

If anyone could tell I'd been crying, they at least didn't say anything about it.

In the end, I was glad that I went to class. The mock group therapy session was a success. I was in awe of how easily I slipped into the role of group therapist, even though I walked into class looking like someone in need of group therapy. One of my classmates told me about the rage room he'd attended, and how the owners were looking to hire a licensed therapist. I left class feeling victorious and content and I promptly fell to pieces the moment I got into my car.

"Leave it to Salem to get cancer again, if only because he missed how spoiled he got during it," I said to Gabe, in between tears, that night. Salem sat regally as I petted him.

There was nothing to do but hold space for the grief and the sorrow—for the unbearable recognition that we hadn't beaten cancer. We'd only bought ourselves time. For the rest of Salem's life, that was exactly what we'd be doing. Expensive chemo, remission, bought time. Lather, rinse, repeat.

Years ago, when Salem's brother, Milo, had to be rushed to the emergency animal hospital, one of the forms requested permission to take additional measures. Gabe wrote in the margins, "Take every measure. Whatever it takes. Don't let my baby die."

I'd thought about that moment countless times since.

I thought about those words now.

Whatever it takes. Don't let my baby die.

I took a double dose of ibuprofen. I rubbed hydrocortisone cream on my face. I had cried myself into an unbearable headache and an eczema outbreak. It was all I could do for myself at that point.

Sometimes self-care looks like triage.

Chapter 19: Mothering

I tried to keep busy. I did home improvement projects. I brought Salem outside with me and hooked him to his leash and let him explore the yard. I scooped him up afterwards and felt him sink into my arms.

"Fine, you're spoiled for the rest of your life," I told him. "Just get better."

The world felt beautiful and empty. I felt enmeshed and detached.

The oncology vet was optimistic. Salem had responded well to his first round of chemo. They predicted that the second round would be just as successful.

Gabe would drive Salem to most of his chemo appointments—much like the first round. I was primarily in charge of Salem's medication—just like the first round.

The only positive to Salem's first cancer diagnosis was that it had created such an all-hands-on deck situation that the lingering pain surrounding Gabe's and my separation was left to wither and die. It forced us to see that we could still work as a team, even though the terms and conditions had radically changed.

(And I tried my best not to give any weight to the idea that Salem got cancer as a response to his parents breaking up.)

THE YEAR OF DATING MYSELF

Salem's cancer solidified May as a month for rest.

One night, I grabbed a book from my to-read pile. I sat in the wicker chair by my bedroom window. I propped my feet up on the windowsill. I opened my book and absorbed the pages. I deliberately picked a collection of essays, in case I had to abandon the book when my summer semester began.

I needed something that didn't carry the weight of obligation.

I was exhausted. My grades for the spring semester had just come in. My 4.0 remained. But it was hard to celebrate.

My phone sat across the room, on my bed. I was behind on my messages. There were entire messaging apps that I hadn't opened in days.

In the pile of unread messages were two men, both wondering when we could hang out. "Innocent" outings, just something fun to do—because, y'know, I'm such a fun person.

It was just a coincidence that they also wished to sleep with me.

There was a third man in my inbox who'd decided that it was the time to remind me that I should consider men that I'd previously "friend zoned."

(Hint: he was talking about himself.)

It had been what made relationship hopping so easy. I always had someone vying for my time. I dove into all these "innocent" opportunities because—what was the worst that could happen?

But, even if I'd wanted to, I couldn't fall back on my old patterns. I was drained. Everything felt overwhelming.

Everyone wanted something. Everyone needed something from me. Everyone was demanding my time, my attention.

I didn't want to deal with the outside world anymore.

I'd just gotten into a tiff with some anonymous man online, who'd told me that women just needed to pick better men—but also, I needed to get off my high horse, stop pretending I was perfect, and stop being so picky.

I was tired. I was tired of juggling everything. I was tired of having to do all this goddamn *healing*. I was tired of having to watch my every word, every time I tried to heal out loud, lest it become fodder for retaliation.

I was tired of feeling like I had to justify my every move. I was tired of feeling like I had to be the perfect victim or else the abuse must've never happened.

I was tired of men fully knowing that I was dating myself and still throwing their names into the ring. I was tired of being reminded that these men *just didn't care* about my boundaries.

I was tired of being told to "pick better" and yet when I said that I was finally picking me, people came out of the woodwork to say I'm bitter, to say, "don't worry the *right man* will come along."

I was tired because earlier that week I had to explain to a guy friend that I didn't have the energy to talk because of everything with Salem—and my supposed friend gave me a flippant response before continuing to talk about *his* problems. When I held firm about my lack of bandwidth, he thought a proper apology was to send me a long-winded text about when *his* cat died.

Two days later he asked if my therapist had figured out why I keep choosing assholes.

It took brute force not to respond with, "it's the same reason why I haven't blocked your number."

I was tired of feeling like my emotions were trivial, but my emotional labor was expected. I was tired of being told (by complete strangers, but most importantly by me) that *it'd been eight months since the relationship ended so why don't I just get over it?*

I was So. Damn. Tired.

I ended up reading only one essay before giving up and going to bed.

Some other night would have to be a cozy reading night. That night, I just had to sit with yet more of my emotions.

I took myself out for coffee Mother's Day morning.

I'd decided to celebrate Mother's Day in my own way. I'd been doing the messy work of re-parenting myself. I'd been devoted to healing my wounded inner child and my wounded inner teenager. I wanted to celebrate my journey. I wanted to celebrate being a mother to myself—the mother I always needed.

I thought about myself as my own mother. Like so many other moms, I hadn't been perfect, but dammit if I hadn't been doing the best with what I had. I thought about my last therapy session. I was struggling to empathize with "teenager me"—until I realized that I wasn't imagining myself as an actual teen. I was envisioning myself in my twenties, the version of me who had "no excuse" to be the way that she was.

Over coffee, I also thought about the conversation I'd had with Gabe, just the day before. There had been a friend's birthday party. Afterward, we had discussed the behavior of some of the partygoers.

"It's a reflection of what they've gone through," said Gabe. "It makes them self-focused."

"I get it. We know how I was in my twenties," I said. "When you're stuck in survival mode, it compromises your ability to recognize the needs of others."

"Oh yeah, people stuck in survival mode," Gabe joked. "The absolute worst!"

"They really are the worst," I said, my serious tone in direct opposition to his jovial tone.

"That was meant to be a joke," he replied, his demeanor noticeably softer. "Like, comedic relief."

"Oh, I know," I said. "But I'm not joking. I wouldn't want to hang out with the version of me from my twenties. She was the worst."

Gabe turned to me with a look of pure resoluteness.

"She was a sweetheart."

Gabe's voice was stern. I was stunned into silence.

She was a sweetheart.

"Don't get me wrong: she was also a pain in the ass," he added. "But her heart was always in the right place."

I didn't know how to respond. It had gotten so easy to vilify that version of me. Look at all the mistakes she'd made! If only she hadn't been so messed up!

"I—I really appreciate that," I stammered out.

I thought about all the times Gabe had called me his "tenderhearted girl." I thought of all the times he told me that I was getting in the way of my own healing by calling myself a monster. The most devastating discovery is realizing your self-hatred was a protective measure—because the alternative would've been unbearable. Hating the version of myself from my twenties shielded me from the unbearable fact that she was trying so hard with such an unwinnable set of cards.

She was a sweet woman—a sweet *girl*, emotionally closer to a teenager—and could never catch a break. That she was flawed and layered and made mistakes, but she wasn't the villain.

She was a *sweetheart.*

She had an innocence about her—an innocence that her once-husband had been (and still was) incredibly protective of.

Some people saw that innocence and saw an easy victim instead, I thought, unsure if what I felt in that moment was grief, rage, or a combination of both.

Twentysomething me had been just as in need of a mother. She'd destroyed herself trying to find one with her actual mother—and

THE YEAR OF DATING MYSELF

she kept trying, no matter how fruitless the attempts were. That version of myself was a sweetheart. I was too busy blaming her for the end of my marriage to see that.

I curled up in my wicker chair again, as Mother's Day drew to a close.

If I could be the mother to the child and teen parts of myself, then I could be the mother to the version of myself in her twenties. I watched the sun set. I imagined the things that younger me went through, and I imagined present-day me as her mother. I imagined being by her side as she planned her wedding, telling her that her father was out of line for pretending he wouldn't attend—that she could walk herself down the aisle, instead of begging a disinterested old man to do it.

I imagined being her listening ear as she talked around her hesitation to have children—and then being there as she realized that she didn't want children at all.

I imagined being the one to explain to her that what that charity director did to her was assault—and no, she didn't "ask for it" because she kept coming back to volunteer. I imagined sitting with her as she realized her marriage was falling apart, as she lamented how she was aware of her patterns but felt powerless to stop them. I sat with her as her father died and she realized there would be no salvation.

In one night, I witnessed a decade of events. I was the mother who showed twentysomething me love when all she could do was hate herself.

I'd learned to love the child version of myself, to fully witness her worthiness. It was time every version of myself got the same.

I thought about texting my brother, wishing my mother a happy Mother's Day by proxy. But I decided against it. She wouldn't remember what my brother said, anyway.

Chapter 20: Back to the Start

I finally returned to hiking.

My goal had been one hike a month. It was a humbling goal: I used to hike twice a week, every week, tackling every hiking challenge, completing some of the hardest trails. It's hard to tell exactly *what* stopped it. I returned to therapy and started grad school in the same year that my hiking dwindled to nothing.

The last time I hiked was New Year's at Arches National Park. Before that, I hadn't done a hike since the previous February. And before that? One during the previous summer.

I used to hike twice a week. That devolved into hiking twice a year. The mountains weren't just calling; they were making note of my absence. It was time to disrupt the truancy.

The trail I decided on was a gentle four miles. A far cry from my extreme hiking days.

"Yes, but extreme hiker Abby wasn't processing her trauma!" I exclaimed sardonically, setting off for the trailhead.

I drove down a state route that I'd driven countless times before, and was quickly reminded of one unfortunate fact: I was going to drive past an ex-boyfriend's house.

THE YEAR OF DATING MYSELF

The ex who'd dumped me twice to reunite with his ex-wife lived on the very road I was on.

Hey, remember when you thought him living on the road to your hikes meant that you two were soulmates? I said wryly to myself.

Sometimes synchronicity—those meaningful coincidences that serve as a divine sign—can be, if nothing else, just a sign you're paying attention.

I rolled my eyes and added, *file under: you will cling to just about anything.*

I was merging onto a rotary when it dawned on me that I'd driven past his house without realizing it.

The hike itself was like getting reacquainted with an old friend: the initial moment of disorientation, enough to make you worry that the spark had faded—only to discover that you're picking up right where you left off.

As I made my way up the mountain—as I focused on the trail and felt something in me settle—a simple thought rose to the surface: I was being unfair to the extreme hiker version of myself.

Did most of her hikes happen in the time period between when she dropped out of therapy and when she returned? Sure.

But that didn't mean she wasn't processing her trauma.

Extreme hiker me disappeared into the woods during some of the hardest years of her life. She went into the woods to survive the aftereffects of her father's death, of the predatory charity director, and of her marriage being on the rocks. She went into the woods to survive the rage, confusion, heartache, and stress. She went into the woods and felt a stillness in her spirit, as if the trees were absorbing her sorrow. She went on those extreme hikes because that was the only way to get her body up to the same level as her anxiety—and then run them both into exhaustion.

But hiking also tapped into something deeper. Extreme hiker me was once little girl me, hiking alongside her parents. Happy childhood memories were few and far between—and they all seemed to happen on the trail. It might not have been in a therapist's office, but I'd been in deep communion with the parts of me that needed healing.

We're constantly doing the best we can with what we have.

The vista from the summit was majestic. I sat down, making myself rest. Extreme hiker me, for all the peace she'd find in the mountains, never stayed at the summit for more than a moment.

For everything she did to keep her head on straight, she was always on the run.

Learning to sit still with what is, instead of chasing after the next thing. It was something she and I both struggled with.

The difference was that I had an obligation to do the best I could with the newer resources I'd been given.

I put that obligation to the test, a few days later, when a song came on my car's radio and my breath caught.

It was one of those Christian pop songs that hides its religious message like the tiniest chopped vegetables in a child's meal. The first time I'd listened to it, I had no clue it was about God. All I heard was a song about remembering someone's worth when they're at their lowest.

And—given where I was when I'd first heard that song—that made sense.

I heard the song for the first time just hours after a heartbreak. It had been my first relationship since my marriage, and the first time since I was nineteen that I'd fallen in love with someone.

THE YEAR OF DATING MYSELF

It had been one of those calamitous relationships. I loved him fiercely, and he was fiercely enthusiastic about it—right up until he realized that actual feelings were on the line. He didn't know how to handle it and reacted with distance, with cruel gestures designed to remind me of where I fit in his priorities. He redefined our relationship—more casual, less romantic—before deciding that the restructuring wouldn't be enough.

Hearing that song again immediately brought me back to that time in my life. I drove aimlessly around, playing the song again, and again, and again, my cheeks soaked with tears. I remembered how quickly I jumped into dating after he broke up with me. I downloaded dating apps for the first time. I went on date after date after date, sometimes two in the same day.

Eventually I found a spark with a man who looked like the brawnier cousin of the man who'd just broken my heart. I latched onto him—and I dismissed how often he brought up his ex-wife, and the look in his eyes when he did.

I never would've taken that brawny man back after the first time he dumped me for his ex-wife, had he not been my bandage love; my replacement for heartbreak. And—had I not been running from the pain of being dumped a second time for the ex-wife—I never would have agreed to a date with the man who had a hammock and a fire pit. I doubt a man from Missouri would've even bothered contacting me, had he not seen everything that I was posting online about the sorrow caused by the man with the hammock. And I truly must believe that my most recent ex would've never had a chance to become a partner in the first place, had I not been in a daze over the Missouri man's actions.

In that unassuming Christian song, I had found my patient zero. The heartbreak that catapulted me feverishly forward, desperate to replace old pain with new love.

I had loved patient zero dearly, and I'd been willing to do anything to avoid facing the loss. But all it did was create new depths to that loss, until I'd hit rock bottom. I pulled into my driveway and continued to cry. Something had just caught up with me, and it was not unlike moving a leg that had fallen asleep.

The only thing left to do was survive the unbearable pins and needles.

Part VI:
June

Chapter 21: Alone, with Cats

I spent the evening convinced that I had strep throat. When the pain went away, I tried to write it off as hay fever. But by the end of the day, it was clear that I didn't need "hay" in front of the word "fever."

I spent the unofficial start to summer laid up in bed. Salem was my constant companion, curled up in one corner, with Milo in the other. Their sister, Artemis, peeved to be sharing space with her brothers, curled up on the floor by my bed. The virus coursing through my system had rendered me useless. The smallest tasks depleted me. I was simultaneously boiling and shivering. I felt like I could feel every single muscle fiber—and every single one ached. I took two tests to make sure I didn't have COVID-19—a ripple effect from the pandemic, the fear that every illness is COVID.

I dozed throughout the day. Eventually, Artemis hopped onto the bed, willing to put up with sharing if it meant she could cuddle into me.

"Good luck being alone with all your cats!"—the proverbial threat, a supposed punishment if a woman is too picky. I'd heard it countless times by that point in my life.

But I thought of my cats' loyal closeness as I burned with fever. I compared it to the last time I was sick, near the end of my last relationship—when I used what little energy I had to placate my boyfriend as he punished me for voicing a concern the night before.

Being single with cats sure beats being alone with a man.

The virus eventually left, but not before giving me a parting gift: laryngitis. I continued to call out from work. I put myself on vocal rest. I reminded myself that I was lucky it hadn't occurred in a few weeks' time. I'd rather have canceled local dates than my flight to Missouri.

Attending St. Louis Pride was slowly becoming a bigger friend event. It was more than just me and Britt flying out to visit Georgia. A large portion of our online community was coming together. A group chat had been created for everyone and a house had been rented for the weekend.

My voice slowly returned. Diane sent me a series of warm-ups to perform for my vocal rehab.

"I really recommend these warm-ups before you do any bit of talking," she advised.

My heart sank at the innocent bit of advice, as I was reminded of one of the lies I never got any truth to.

While we were still together, my ex landed a part in a community theater production. I went down to see him on opening weekend. I attended the Friday and Saturday shows, but he told me that the matinee was already sold out—and, furthermore, he would have to leave for the matinee two hours early for extra vocal warm-ups, since matinees are earlier in the day and his vocal cords would have less time to "naturally" warm up with talking.

I knew, deep down, it was all a lie. The show's website showed a half-empty theater for Sunday—and even I knew no performer needs two hours of warmups, let alone two *additional* hours. The same way I knew something was up when he parked outside his apartment after the show but didn't come in for another forty-five minutes.

After the breakup, I found out about the local women he was dating, on top of the countless women online. The clues painted a clear enough picture. But it still bothered me that I didn't have definitive answers and concrete proof.

Sometimes one of the hardest pills to swallow is that you will never get the full truth. There will always be lies left uncovered. There will always be secrets you'll never find out. It doesn't matter how hard you try to get to the bottom of things; you're navigating a bottomless pit.

And that gnawing reality can drive you to the point of madness.

I got my voice back in time to see my favorite band again, this time with Lindsey and their partner—but my plans almost got upended thanks to a baby bird in the middle of the road.

I got out of my car and started walking to the baby bird. It stood up and started running away, its little stubs for wings flared out to the sides. I did my best to corral the baby bird, flanking it so it had no choice but to get onto the grass. Once it scuttled into a small patch of forest, I wished it good luck and got back into my car.

"My desire to fix the broken baby birds of the world just got literal," I said to myself as I continued my drive.

A part of me had wanted to cancel my plans and tend to the bird, but I was grateful I didn't. The concert was an incredible experience. We spent the night jamming out to our favorite songs. To avoid angering my vocal cords, I silently mouthed the lyrics—a karmic penance after shouting the lyrics at the last concert. It was an unforgettable time, one I'm glad that I didn't let my little bleeding heart get in the way of.

THE YEAR OF DATING MYSELF

As I drove home, I couldn't help but think of the baby bird. I hoped their mother had found them. I reminded myself that it was not my job to upend my life and take care of the broken baby birds of the world.

Especially since most of them aren't broken at all. They just need to grow up.

Chapter 22: Laugh Where You Cried

It took me until June to finally take myself out to dinner at a sit-down restaurant.

I was still anxious about dining alone. That hesitation was why I'd missed out on the cuisine while I visited Québec City.

(But, to give myself grace, I was also in a frenetic headspace, back then. Who knows what it would've been like, had I left that abusive relationship *before* going on my first solo trip?)

As I sat at a table designed for four, I felt the opposite of anxious. I felt empowered. The entire table was for me. My table was my reminder that I was allowed to take up space.

After my dinner, I started packing for St. Louis Pride.

"Remember the last time I packed for Missouri?" I said to Georgia.

"Laugh in the places we cried," Georgia replied.

I'd only been to Missouri one other time—to visit the man who'd spent months romancing me, only to violate my boundaries and my ability to consent when I came out to see him. I was in such a daze about the experience that it took months to realize what had happened. Months—and eventually learning that it was his pattern, that he'd harmed other women in the exact same way.

I was ready to laugh in a place where I'd cried—even though, technically, the only tears I'd shed in Missouri were at the airport as I waited for my flight back home. Back then, I thought I was crying because I wasn't ready to leave; but, in retrospect, I wondered what else could've been rumbling below the surface that was reducing me to tears.

I'd almost forgotten about Father's Day. Someone mentioned it in passing and the only response I had was, "Huh, it's today, isn't it?"

I spent Father's Day doing yardwork. Pulling weeds, mowing lawns, digging up shrubs.

There was a lot to do to correct the neglect from the previous year, when I'd been too busy driving three states over to see my then-boyfriend. Nature wasted no time proving how quickly it will reclaim things. But it was work I did happily. I thought of how close I'd been to leaving that house—leaving my friends, a job I loved, my community, my education—to move in with a man who'd sold me a false bill of romantic goods. Narrowly missing what would've been one of the worst mistakes of my life felt like being pulled back onto the sidewalk right as a bus rushes by. You surge with hysterical gratitude.

I couldn't help but ruminate about Father's Day. It was closing in on the eight-year anniversary of my father's death. In those eight years, I'd gone to countless support group meetings for people whose lives had been impacted by a loved one's struggles with alcohol. I'd filled volumes of journals. I'd hiked every hikeable peak. I'd gone in and out of therapy. I started EMDR.

Eight years of hard work, but I was finally at peace with who my father was. I could hold two things true at the same time: that his upbringing was heartbreaking, and that it didn't excuse making my upbringing equally so. I could see the little boy, terrorized by his father—and I could see the little girl, also terrorized by her father.

I thought about that forced forgiveness I'd given, at my father's deathbed. I'd later realize that the forced forgiveness had hindered my ability to actually heal. It was nearly a decade later that I could say that I'd forgiven him, and it wasn't a lie.

Sometimes forgiveness isn't the launchpad for healing, but the byproduct of it. Sometimes forgiveness is what you find amidst the ashes when you've burned through all your rage.

Chapter 23: Pride

I'd learned my lesson from Vegas and showed up for my flight to St. Louis two hours early.

In an ironic twist, I got to the airport with zero issues—except for a delayed flight.

The group chat was alive with anticipation. Britt and Georgia were already there. Others would be arriving shortly after. Eventually, my flight was ready for takeoff. I breathed a sigh of relief and got ready to return to Missouri. When I touched down, Georgia came to pick me up, with Britt in the passenger seat. I wrapped them both in tight hugs and gleefully got ready for our first adventure.

I was relieved with how little I thought about my last visit to that city. We welcomed the other people as they arrived before spending the evening at a dinner theater.

St. Louis Pride was a wonderful, dizzying experience. It was my first Pride event, and I finally understood what it meant to be in complete celebration of oneself. The friend group spent the first night talking until two in the morning, and the next evening at a comedy show. Everything felt surreal, yet familiar. We all clicked as if we'd known each other our whole lives. I got a glimpse into what life could be like inside a community.

THE YEAR OF DATING MYSELF

But I could tell something was up on Sunday evening. There was an exhaustion in me that I couldn't blame on the long days and little sleep. I went to bed convinced it would go away with a full night's rest—that I was *fine* and I'd be better in the morning. But I spiked a fever during the night and woke up drenched in sweat. The muscle aches were so bad that I started whimpering.

"At least my flight is a direct flight," I said, optimistically. Britt wasn't feeling great either.

I put on a surgical mask for the airport and counted down the minutes until I was in my bed. My flight was only two hours long. Including my drive, I'd be home by the early evening at the latest.

. . . And then the first delay happened.

The airline attendant explained that the Federal Aviation Administration was limiting flights, thanks to a patch of severe weather. Our flight got pushed out an additional hour. I did my best to think positively. I snuck off into the bathroom to blow my nose—the only time I felt safe enough to pull down my mask.

We finally boarded and got ready for liftoff. The plane pulled away from the jetway—and then stopped. The pilot came on the speaker system to inform us that, because the weather patch stood directly in between us and Boston, our flight was to be rerouted.

"There's a storm front that's covering our flight path," said the pilot. "Everything is being diverted. Our new flight time will be a little over three and a half hours. We are currently waiting for the FAA to give us the go ahead."

I became acutely aware of my breath as we sat on the tarmac for an additional hour and a half. It was hard not to spiral out. If there were ever a flight that I needed to go right, it was that one. We were taking off at the time we were supposed to have landed. If I was lucky, I'd get home by midnight.

Eventually the plane started moving and we took off. I gritted my teeth as we ascended, the changing air pressure hitting my ear drums like an ice pick. I fruitlessly tried moving my jaw to get my ears to pop. I was a wreck. I tried to get some rest, but I couldn't get comfortable. Everything ached. The hours that ticked by plucked at my guilt for being sick while on an airplane. I felt like a plague rat. My nose was running and I had no tissues. My mask became sodden, making it even harder to breathe.

The plane rose and lowered in altitude multiple times—and my sinuses felt every foot of elevation change. We arrived in the Boston area, only to circle the city and continue our pattern of ascension and descension. The only upside to the unbearable ice pick feeling in my ears was that it drowned out how raw the tip of my nose had become.

We landed after 11 p.m. I took the shuttle bus to the subway, then the train to my car. The air was thick and hot, and I was shivering. I drove home in a near delirium.

I got home after one in the morning.

I trudged up my stairs and collapsed into bed.

I had *just* recovered from being sick. I'd been laid out for days— and then without a voice for two weeks. I was frustrated. I felt held back, like I was constantly on a delay. I slept the soundest that I'd had in days and woke up feeling like I'd been hit by a bus.

I took an at-home COVID test, convinced it would be negative, just like before. I was going on three years without once catching it. I was convinced that I'd forever stay lucky, forever a member of the club of people who never had the virus. The at-home tests are supposed to take fifteen minutes, but it only took five minutes before the second line appeared: bold and red, and digging its heels in about its arrival.

Well, shit.

That wasn't expected.

My luck had run out, after all.

It was COVID.

Part VII: July

Chapter 24: Reassurance

I spent the next few days in and out of consciousness. The virus navigated an identity crisis in my body, not sure exactly which version it wanted to be. It started with phlegmy coughs, only to switch to dry. One day it was the unbearable muscle aches; the next, asthmatic breathing.

The group chat became all about testing. Georgia was first asymptomatic before getting symptoms as bad as mine. Britt's symptoms mercifully stayed level. Everyone else was negative.

We began to do the math on who could've given it to us. I didn't say it out loud, because I didn't want it to be true—but all I could think of was the taxi driver who'd brought us across town, before the rest of the group arrived. A lovely, soft-spoken woman who'd carted the three of us, and listened as we spent that half-hour taxi ride comparing notes on our abusive exes. When we arrived at our rental, Britt apologized to the driver for having to listen to our trauma.

"It's not a problem at all," the driver said, before giving a knowing smile and adding: "We're all women."

A small, subtle nod to the ubiquity of it all—to the universal suffering some women face at the hands of abusive men. Every woman I knew had at least one harrowing tale to share.

As I slowly recovered from COVID, I tried my best to get through my schoolwork, even though the brain fog was otherworldly. I went outside when I could, taking in the fresh air. I also got my tickets with Lana to go to Philadelphia, her hometown, at the end of the month.

I focused on that trip; I needed to. Thanks to COVID-19, I had canceled my Fourth of July plans, which only highlighted just how many potential dates I'd yet to attempt, thanks to constantly getting sick. I was returning to Pennsylvania at the end of the month. Britt was going to drive up and join us—and two of my platonic soulmates were finally going to meet each other.

At that moment, that was enough for me. It had to be.

I drove home from work a few weeks later, and learned exactly what it felt like to smile a beaming smile and clench your teeth at the same time.

"Dammit, I have a crush," I said to Danielle.

The crush was a kind-eyed clinician at the drug rehab program where I worked part-time, running mind-body coping skills groups.

"With a *guy*," I continued. "And—right after Pride? This feels biphobic."

It was impossible at that point to deny it. He was one of the men who'd given me those "squishy" feelings—the kind that looked like a crush if you squinted at it right—but it was evolving. I got excited when he was there; disappointed when he wasn't. It'd become hard to look him in the eyes without my face flushing.

The realization that I had a full-on crush came in two parts: the first, when I found myself wondering what it'd be like to kiss him and felt something surge through me. The second happened earlier that day, when I'd said goodbye and his eyes were the last thing I saw before the elevator doors closed and I bit my lip in response.

Dammit.

I have a crush.

"I'm not going to do anything with it," I told Danielle. "I'm dating myself right now, and I'm not about to cheat on me."

Part of me wanted to exorcize the crush—figure out some way to remove it like cutting off the moldy parts of bread. But cutting off the visible mold doesn't make the bread mold-free. The mold has already infiltrated the entire loaf. The only course of action I had was to turn directly into the waves. I could let myself imagine his kiss while knowing I wasn't going to seek it out.

I tried to remind myself that my feelings were something to be celebrated. They were a reassurance. After my experience with the Missouri man, I'd told a friend that he'd rendered me incapable of both sexual and romantic desire.

"I won't invalidate the asexuality," she said. "But I can't imagine someone like you being aromantic for the rest of your life."

I had to wonder if it was, in part, why I'd been so quick to replace old pain with new love. I couldn't bear the idea of the hopeless romantic in me dying, so I'd latch onto the first man who could make that side of me feel alive.

I wasn't going to abandon my Solo Tour just to resuscitate my romantic heart. But, in the safety of my mind, as I continued to learn to latch onto myself, I could allow those butterflies, the echoes of reassurance that my heart still beats, despite how many times it'd been broken.

Chapter 25: The Longest Week

"I appreciate you not burying the lead," my therapist said, when I sat down on her couch and the first words out of my mouth were, "my ex inadvertently exposed himself as an abuser."

"Now we're going to need backstory."

But where to begin?

It started with a social media influencer revealing his problematic attitudes toward women and the online community taking him to task for it. Britt's name got dragged into the mix as the influencer claimed that he'd talked to her and that she supported him. She was quick to expose the lie. She didn't mince words as she talked about how so many guys claim to be feminists when, in reality, they're terrible to women. Britt also directed some jabs at my ex, a few nods that she was onto him too. My ex was quick to use every tactic in the book to intimidate Britt. His intimidation tactics worked for a moment, before she told him to stand down because she knew how abusive he'd been to women. Instead of standing down, he tried to prove how good he was—only to prove the opposite.

He published screenshots of my text messages with him, heavily insinuating that I was crazy. But all the texts revealed was that my spirit had been broken; that I was walking on eggshells and apologizing for my every word.

And his audience saw it too.

"People are calling him *out*," Stella exclaimed as she shared the news. "There are people in his comments section like, 'you sound like my abusive ex.'"

He deleted the post and made another one, that time apologizing, hinting that he *used to be* a bad guy, but *now* he's reformed.

He took the post down within an hour.

"He isn't doing what he thinks he's doing," said Stella.

I was vindicated. The days of worrying that I'd be found guilty in the court of public opinion of being the bitter, psycho ex were over. It wasn't until that evening that I even remembered that I had my genetic counseling appointment in the morning.

How dizzying life is when one gigantic event is overshadowed by another.

Britt said that she'd reveal proof of his abusive history and she was ready to call his bluff. I sent Britt the proof I had as well as evidence from other women. I logged offline and went to bed early and slept the sleep of someone who'd been retraumatized, but had also been validated in their trauma.

I was on my drive to the genetic counselor when Britt called.

"So, change of plans," Britt said, her voice clipped.

Something was up.

"What happened?"

"So, someone reached out to me, someone who used to be friends with your ex . . ."

As I pulled into the hospital parking lot, Britt dropped a bombshell on me.

"A few years ago, he slept with a seventeen-year-old that was in the same production as him. He was around thirty when it happened."

I turned off my car and sat back, speechless.

It's an indescribable feeling, when you've been handed the biggest smoking gun, but it's so revolting that you don't want to touch it, let alone hold it.

I wanted to stay on the phone with Britt, but I had to go in for my appointment.

I checked in, found a seat, and texted Danielle the update.

"This is why he couldn't ignore Britt," said Danielle. "This is why he tried to shut her down. The same way he tried to shut you down. He knew what skeletons were in his closet. He knew what would happen if things were exposed."

I wanted to reply, but my name was called at that very moment. Perhaps it was a blessing, juggling the new information right before my genetic appointment. I could only imagine the anxiety I would've felt otherwise, sitting in the lobby with the full weight of early onset Alzheimer's on my shoulders. Likewise, I could only imagine the state I would've been in, if I'd been given time to stew on the most recent development.

Sometimes it's an act of mercy to be overloaded.

I followed the counselor into an exam room and told her my situation.

"The smartest move would be to test your mother," she said. "She'd qualify for free genetic testing. This might be a family decision to be addressed before we do anything else."

I tried to hide my smirk and failed miserably. *Oh. Yeah. People have families—families that they make decisions together with.*

The alternative was for me to get genetic testing done, which was what I wanted all along. It would cost $250, out of pocket.

"Compared to the labs my primary care doctor had found, that's a bargain," I said.

She prepared the sample kit and I swabbed my cheeks.

"You should get the results in about a month," said the counselor. I thanked the counselor for her time while my phone kept buzzing from my purse.

I left my appointment, got in my car, and deflated. I grabbed my steering wheel, leaned my head against my hands, and sighed. I forced myself to sit upright and drove myself home. Off in the distance, storm clouds were approaching.

During my appointment, Britt published her post, revealing the secret about the seventeen-year-old. My ex responded to the video by deactivating his online platforms.

I drove home, sat in my kitchen, and listened to the rainfall.

I watched the downpour. I let out a sigh and the words, "I'm so tired," slipped out of my mouth.

The words held truth that I wasn't ready to admit.

I felt a bubble burst.

"I don't want to do this anymore," I continued, deliberately saying what I was afraid to hold space for.

And then I broke down crying.

The next day I stayed offline.

In my basement sat an inflatable rowboat, one that'd been gathering dust for years. I'd purchased it the summer before my father passed away, when the world felt hazy and unreal. My father had a similar inflatable rowboat, back when I was a child. I'd purchased mine, thinking it would cheer me up.

It stayed in my basement instead.

I gathered what I needed. There was a pond just down the street from me, perfect for my excursion. I grabbed the unopened box—

the dust on it grimy and sticky—and tossed it in my car. I didn't have the energy to test out the boat beforehand.

I parked at the pond, opened the box, and began inflating the boat. I was grateful to see that it held up. It was as if I'd purchased it that day, new rubber smell and all. I cast myself off into the pond and began rowing.

I didn't ponder about my father, or my ex, or the events of the last few days.

I simply rowed.

I listened to the birds chirping. I listened to the sound of the water as my paddles hit the surface. I felt the sun on my skin. I pulled up my oars and floated. The same way the wounded child part of me finally felt safe, the wounded girlfriend part of me finally did too. She didn't have to be on guard anymore.

She was *free*.

I slowly rowed back to shore. I was humbled by how exhausted I was. I didn't have the same stamina that I once did, as a child. I was certainly stronger, but I tired more easily.

There's a metaphor there, somewhere.

I got home and continued to stay offline. I watched a few episodes of a TV series that I'd fallen in love with—a show about two divorced women in their seventies, who proved that friendship will always be the most important bond in our lives. I fell asleep early. All the parts of me that had been on alert were finally telling me how exhausted they'd been, all along.

Finally being able to stand in your truth means having to listen to the truth about your limits—and lay down.

"Did we get good news?" I asked Gabe, after Salem's oncology appointment.

Salem had been responding well to chemo again and was 75 percent finished with treatment.

"We got amazing news," he replied. "The ultrasound found zero masses in his stomach."

"He's cancer free?"

"Effectively so, yes."

Sometimes things just seem to come together, all at once. Maybe they're not happy endings, per se, but they're moments of reprieve, moments that fill your cup with hope, moments that make you believe it's all going to be okay.

Salem was in better shape at the 3/4 mark than he was at the end of his first chemotherapy treatment.

There was hope.

Maybe it would all be okay.

I knew I was lucky. The same way most cats with stomach cancer don't see a second remission, most abuse survivors don't get any other option but to move on in silent suffering.

The year was half over, and I already had enough adventure to fill a few books.

But heaven knows, I was *tired*. I didn't want to have any more chapters like the previous ones. I was tired of all these plot twists, the series-long villains.

I just wanted peace.

Sometimes vindication comes at a price. Sometimes progress takes its toll. The spark of adventure burns us to ashes. There's nothing wrong with wanting to slow down, if only to catch our breath.

It's okay to say you're tired—that you don't want to keep up that pace anymore.

Chapter 26: Philadelphia

Britt called me a few days before my flight to Philadelphia with Lana.

"I don't want you to panic, but . . ." Britt began, and I immediately panicked. "I just got the most unnerving email."

"What?"

"Guess who sent me a cease and desist."

I checked my email and found that I had one too. I stopped breathing as I looked at all the legal jargon, the threats, the six-figure sum's worth of damages I'd reportedly caused my ex-boyfriend.

"He's seriously threatening to sue us?"

I forced myself to take a deep breath. I contacted a few of my legal friends. I talked through it with Britt. We pushed past the immediate fear and studied the email in front of us.

The more we dissected it, the more absurd it became. We went through the list of allegations. At the very top of the list: alleging that he doesn't go to therapy, that he cheated on me, that he was emotionally abusive to me. It was comical, in a way, to see such things listed out. There was a "settlement deal" with a lengthy yet vague list of demands. Our legal friends helped point out holes in the document, and how it looked like a poorly copied template, designed to make us scared, but ultimately nonsensical. The panic slowly dissolved into laughter. The email lost its bullying presence; there was a silliness to it.

It's amazing how many monsters turn out to be nothing but shadows when stared down.

We decided that the best course of action was to ignore his email. At the end of the day, the cease and desist was redundant: after Britt's video, we'd already *ceased* and *desisted* talking about him. We'd spoken our peace, and there was nothing more we wanted to say. The once-menacing email looked like a tantruming boy, threatening to throw his classmates in jail for infinity years.

And we were over childish games.

Despite the eventful days prior, my flight to Philadelphia went smoothly—as did the trip itself. Britt, Lana, and I spent Saturday at an amusement park, beating the brutal summer heat and riding the intense roller coasters. I watched with glee as Lana and Britt became instant friends. There's worry when your close friends from different social circles meet for the first time—if there'll be the same platonic chemistry that had drawn you, individually, to each person. But I watched a kinship form in moments.

When we'd first planned our trip to the theme park, I'd remarked on how much of a "corrective" experience it was going to be, since the last time I'd been to an amusement park was with my ex. Yet, on the actual day of our trip, I thought little of it. A lifetime's worth had happened between those initial plans and their implementation—and I was living a new, different life.

Corrective experiences can be like stitches for a gash that won't close. But for a wound that's healing, perhaps what's needed acts more like an ointment: there to aid in the efforts, but in a way that absorbs into the skin as you carry on with life.

Lana, Britt, and I watched the late-night fireworks show that had once been a staple of Lana's childhood. I watched the lights bounce off the cliff sides and remembered that, thanks to COVID-19, I never got to enjoy Fourth of July fireworks.

But there I was, getting a better show than I would've gotten at any local celebration.

That was a far more impactful corrective experience.

The next day, we visited a museum where I found an Irishman who had my maiden name on the list of fallen soldiers in the American Revolution. I texted my younger brother about it, musing if the soldier had any relation to us.

"Maybe a distant cousin," my brother answered.

Our simple exchange produced a pang in my heart—a hint of what it might feel like when family is a point of connection.

Sometimes you don't fully realize what you missed out on until you get a taste of it.

Monday morning came too soon, and before the noontime sun hit, I was already on my flight back home. Lana was staying an additional week with her family, but I'd already taken off as much time as I could. The summer semester for school was winding down and major projects were due.

I tried to work on those projects during my flight, but I kept nodding off, my head bobbing against the airplane window. I was exhausted; not just from the trip, but from *everything*. Danielle had been ready to go to bat for me, to tell the world that my ex was using the legal system to intimidate Britt and me. All she needed was the go-ahead—but I didn't have it in me to give the green light.

I was so *tired*. I didn't have it in me anymore.

THE YEAR OF DATING MYSELF

I had good things going on in my life. There was delicate beauty in my hand; I feared I would crush it. Sometimes hope looks like a car rolling forward when it's run out of gas—but you've also taken your foot off the brake.

Chapter 27: Ongoing

Sometimes you're given an intervention, just when things feel too big for you to handle.

My newfound crush stopped being fun and began filling me with anxious, uncertain hope.

Yes, I was dating *myself*, but what about *after* the year was over?

What if that guy was the *right guy*, after all?

What if I didn't have to just *imagine* what it was like to kiss him?

I was quick to counter the voice in my head. If he really was the "right guy," then I could keep going about my Solo Tour and the stars would eventually align.

It did little to stop that voice—because that voice was an off-shoot of a much bigger monster: my addictive personality.

I was my father's daughter, after all, and I'd spent my life taking in near-lethal doses of one specific intoxicating substance: romance.

That addictive side was getting a foothold. It tacked on a sense of urgency—*the turnover rate is high for counselors there. What if he's gone before the year is done? What if you lose your chance?*

THE YEAR OF DATING MYSELF

I walked into the rehab facility to run my skills group and my gaze immediately darted to his office. I was deflated to see he wasn't there. Minutes later, someone mentioned his name and my heart fluttered.

I felt unhinged. What was the point of my crush if I was going to act like that? I was supposed to enjoy the butterflies, not treat them like a swarm of locusts.

"Someone lobotomize me," I texted Lana.

Eventually, my crush returned to his office. I could hear him having a conversation with someone, their voices wafting into the hallway. I couldn't make out exactly what the conversation was about, but my ears perked up when I heard:

". . . and that's why my girlfriend now drops off the stuff at . . ."

My ears perked up, but my shoulders relaxed down. Dashed hope never felt so soft.

I finished my work and got ready to leave. I surreptitiously looked over at him as the elevator doors closed. He was still devastatingly cute, even if my face wasn't flushing red over it anymore.

I'd wager it's a small list of people who are happy to learn that their crush is off the market. But it was news that I desperately needed, like I'd been cut off from the drink I kept ordering at the bar.

Finding myself on the edge of such a spiral was sobering. The pattern was too familiar. It made me wonder how many times my father thought, *one drink wouldn't hurt*, before getting blackout drunk.

The experience had just told me, in no uncertain terms, that I wasn't in a place where I could have "just *one* drink."

It made me wonder if I ever would be.

The fervor from the morning had collapsed, and it felt like hearing your voice echo off the walls of an empty apartment. I was coming down from a high that I didn't even want to be on. The "squishy" feelings, in such a short amount of time, had dissipated. The thought of his embrace no longer held me spellbound.

There was relief, but something also felt hollow. It made me think of every person in recovery who wonders if they'll ever experience intense joy again—or if the world will always be a little muted from there on out.

A week after I gave my inflatable rowboat its long-awaited maiden voyage, I found myself in the same section of the grocery store in which I originally found it. But instead of a rowboat, I was looking at a plastic water slide. I picked it up and put it in my cart. It felt right to get it. It felt like a continuation: that, yes, I finally made good on my plans for the rowboat, but the story wasn't going to end there.

It was ongoing—and always would be ongoing.

I'd always be making childlike promises to myself that deserve to be fulfilled.

Chapter 28: Threat

Britt alerted me to the second email.

What exactly had motivated it, I can never say for certain—but, less than a week after the first cease and desist, we received a second one, threatening to not only sue, but press charges.

"That makes literally no sense," I said, feeling the panic rise in me. "He has no case. We haven't even been talking about him."

Britt said she was going to contact her lawyer. I got on the phone with Danielle, trying my best not to cry before allowing the tears to fall.

"It doesn't feel like it, but this is a good thing," said Danielle. "Because now I know what I'm going to say when I talk about him. Anything that I might've said beforehand wouldn't have had this energy. But he's crossed a line. This will not end well for him."

As Danielle prepared her post, I gave her whatever information I could. Danielle sent me the draft of it and I felt something settle in my soul. In her post, Danielle calmly but sternly laid out the facts at hand: that he'd attempted an apology, ran when it didn't work, and then threatened women via the legal system. A few other content creators followed suit, speaking out about the situation and how common it was for the legal system to be used as an intimidation tactic against victims.

"Something has shifted," I told Britt on the phone. "Like, I'm reminded that I'm not fighting this by myself—"

My throat caught. Big, violent tears spilled from my eyes, missing my cheeks entirely. A new set welled up and streamed down my face.

I spent so much of my life with no one truly in my corner. Gabe was the first person to give that to me, and I'd clung desperately to that, even when our marriage was falling apart. But there were multiple people consistently in my corner. I had support and love and kinship. Things had gotten tough and the people in my life had offered me shelter from the storm.

It was never my fight to fight *alone*.

There is nothing as shatteringly beautiful as the realization that you can finally put down your weapon.

I took myself on a coffee date the next morning. I went to the same lake as I had during the winter. I sat on the same bench. To my right, a toddler was simultaneously feeding and chasing a group of ducks.

I took in a few easy breaths. The serenity of it all was too much to bear.

I spent the afternoon in my hammock. I grilled myself a summertime feast, with ice cream for dessert. I went to bed with the ease that comes after spending the day in halcyon rapture with your beloved.

The next day was not only the last day of July, but the deadline for us to comply with my ex's "settlement" demands, lest he press charges. I decided to spend the day hiking.

I chose a route I once took with a man I'd briefly dated—a sweet guy whose undue confidence in his hiking acumen had almost led to our demise (and my *actual* hiking acumen got us back to our cars). I didn't need a corrective experience for it, but I couldn't help but think about that hike with the confident man.

I'd deferred to his judgment, despite it going against my hard-earned wisdom. I remember how we stayed at the mountaintop, despite the storm clouds rolling in—and how he dismissed my requests to leave. When the rain came, he took off running, taking a wrong turn while assuring me we were on the right path. But when the rain cleared up enough for me to check GPS, we were already halfway to the next mountain on the range, with the sun rapidly setting. It took me standing firm in my knowledge for us to safely get down the mountain and back to our cars.

The past version of me would've submitted to the cease and desists. My ex knew I'd been that kind of doormat, and he assumed that he'd get me to return to that—if not during the relationship, then after.

But he never could.

I think that was part of why he'd gotten so nasty with me. The women he picked were not *supposed* to stand up for themselves. He thought he knew what kind of woman I was. He thought he had one who he could manipulate and intimidate into submission.

He thought wrong.

I finished my hike just as the skies changed and the rain came in.

Life is poetry with its subtle nods to the past.

I drove home and promptly fell asleep. I'd been reminded of my strength. But strength must be met with rest, lest something burn out.

Part VIII: August

Chapter 29: It's Okay to Suck

I held my breath in the days following the deadline. I braced myself every time I checked my email. I had a plan in place—including friends from the legal world, ready to help should anything arise—but I desperately hoped I wouldn't have to make good on their offers.

I did my best to find reassurance in the silence. I knew my ex's patterns. Those emails were the immediate bellows from his fits of rage. But when the echoes started to reverberate back, he ran before the sounds could catch up to him. The people he harmed were then left to deal with the noise alone. But echoes fade away—and I could only hope that he would too.

Amidst that, I reached out to a tattoo artist, describing the homage to the Greek goddess Artemis that I passionately wanted. I made a haircut appointment for the first time in a year.

I also made a reservation at an ax throwing studio.

It felt like just the kind of date I'd like, something outside of my comfort zone. I showed up to the studio and the owner gave me a quick tour before showing me to my alley.

"Is this your first time?" he asked.

"It is."

THE YEAR OF DATING MYSELF

"Okay, let me show you a few basic throws," he said, and walked me through how to throw with two arms, and then with one.

"I have Crystal and Reggie here," said the owner, pointing to his employees. "They'll be able to help you out. They'll come over if they hear the axes hitting the ground too often."

My pulse quickened. *Note to self: don't let your axes hit the ground.*

I thanked him and got ready for my first throw. The hatchet barely connected with the wood, but I'd hit a near bullseye.

"Was that your first throw?" Crystal asked.

"It was!" I beamed.

"Good job!"

I bit my lip to hide my smile and grabbed my ax.

"Maybe I should start keeping score," I mused to myself, and threw again.

The ax bounced off the wood and clattered to the floor.

I picked it up and tried again. The ax bounced again. I tried another time, and watched it repeat the same fate.

"Let's see if we can fix that," said Crystal, coming over. I grinned sheepishly as she walked me through the basics again until my ax connected with the board.

I methodically thought out each step as I threw. I missed the board two more times before finally connecting. I continued the mediocre ax throwing waltz—hit, two, three, hit, two, three—before Reggie came over.

"You keep flicking your wrist, like you're doing a free throw," he said. "I imagine the muscle memory is hard to overcome."

I just nodded. People assumed I played basketball because of my height. I didn't, but it was not going to be a time that I corrected anyone.

Reggie gave me a few pointers. Crystal came by and noted that I had more success with the two-handed throw than the one-handed throw. My face flushed red with embarrassment. I had both employees trying to help me in my mediocrity. Eventually, I got the hang of the two-handed throw. I knew I could just continue with the two-handed throw and spare my self-esteem.

But that wasn't why I was doing it, was it?

I switched to the one-handed throw and watched my batting average plummet. Miss after miss after miss.

"I can tell you won't leave here without getting that one-handed throw in, too, huh!" Reggie joked, coming over to help me again. I went back to the two-handed throw, needing some kind of confidence boost if I were going to survive the rest of my date. I went back to the one-handed throw in the last fifteen minutes, telling myself that all I needed was one good throw, and I could call it.

Reggie came by again to give me a few more pointers. I did my best not to let embarrassment cloud my judgment and I went to work. I'd hit the board with one throw, then miss with the next. I told myself that a 50 percent success rate was impressive enough for my first time. I didn't have to be perfect. It was unfair to expect as much.

With a few minutes left, I did a final one-handed throw. My ax connected perfectly with the board; it wasn't a bullseye, but it was close enough. There was my one, good, throw.

"Let's end it on a high note," I said to myself, breathless. I returned my ax to its slot, said goodbye to Crystal and Reggie, and made my way out.

I had humbled myself with ax throwing, but I was also proud of myself. I had a nasty habit of expecting mastery on the first try. Anything short of perfection was met with despair. But that day, I'd let myself be bad. Not only that, but I let myself be bad *in front of other people*. People who knew what they were doing, no less.

I showed myself that the world doesn't end just because I wasn't perfect.

THE YEAR OF DATING MYSELF

I felt new inspiration for my solo dates. I wanted classes for things that I'd never done before—things that I couldn't guarantee I'd be good at. I signed up for pottery and wood crafting classes, for later in the month. I thought about what else I could try.

"I have an idea!" Lana offered when I told her my plans. "You could try fencing! I took a few classes after Samuel passed away."

My heart felt heavy and motivated.

"I'm looking them up as we speak," I responded. "And I'm going to do it in Samuel's honor."

My throat caught. I didn't realize what I was saying until I said it.

Samuel had been Lana's partner a long time ago. The love between them had been the kind that storybooks were made of. But Samuel had gotten sick and couldn't recover. He fought the illness with everything he could, with Lana by his side. It was a battle he ultimately lost.

I knew I had to find a class on fencing. I remembered how valiantly Lana lived afterward, in his memory. The way she expanded in her life to honor the one that was gone.

My Solo Tour, my Year of Dating Myself—it wasn't a new concept. It took effort not to minimize my situation, but it helped remind me that there's something embedded in the hearts of people who felt their chests crack open.

We strive to find what we lost, to shine in response to what dulled our sparkle.

Perhaps it's human nature to grow where circumstances had once demanded we shrink. It wasn't just about solo date nights— or mediocre ax throwing.

It was about proving the stubborn resiliency of the human spirit.

So, by God, I had to find myself a fencing class.

Chapter 30: Something's Fixed, Something's Broken

With a picnic in hand, I drove down to Boston to enjoy Free Shakespeare on the Common. Each summer hosts a Shakespeare performance in the middle of Boston's biggest public park. It was once a ritual of mine when I lived in Boston. I was returning after years away—and by myself, for the first time.

I arrived early and rolled out my beach towel—my stand-in for a picnic blanket. I spent the afternoon soaking in the sun, watching as the Common slowly filled with people. By nightfall, the stage came alive with their rendition of *Macbeth*.

It took until the end of the show to realize that *Macbeth* was the perfect Shakespeare play. *Macbeth*: a cautionary tale, warning that, if you get to the top with misdeeds, your misdeeds will catch up with you. You will never be able to wash your hands of them.

And the more you try to cover up your crimes, the more you've sealed your fate.

I had imagined how things would go when I received my genetic testing results. A letter in my trembling hands, reading my results with tears of relief or tears of sorrow. A phone call, biting my lip

THE YEAR OF DATING MYSELF

as I got the best (or worst) news of my life. I imagined a moment of profound emotion. Finally, the answers I'd been trying to get all year, the end of a long journey.

Reality is never the same as fantasy, but sometimes reality stands in such stark contrast that you don't know what to make of it.

I was in the middle of an all-day seminar for school—the last push of the summer semester—when I checked my email.

While the professor read an excerpt from her presentation slides, I opened one from the hospital.

Attached are the results from your genetic testing for early onset Alzheimer's disease, the message read. *The testing was negative for all three proteins.*

Oh.

I read the line again. I opened the test results and read its contents.

Oh.

I don't have early onset Alzheimer's.

My matter-of-fact response took me by surprise. Only the split-second surge that went through my body gave a hint that the information was important.

I was in a disconnected state. I spent my lunch break texting everyone, saying repeatedly, "I don't have early onset Alzheimer's."

I'd read the line back to myself and the closest I got to an emotional reaction was a slight lump in my throat.

I tried to reassure myself. I was in the middle of a seminar, after all—not the most welcoming place to have a breakdown. Surely when I had time to sit with the news, I'd truly feel what that surge had hinted at.

But as I drove home that evening, using the hour commute to sit in silence and take in what I'd learned, there was only one thing I felt: Grief.

Grief that I couldn't feel anything about the news.

A few tears fell as I drove down the highway. Tears for the fact that I'd been robbed. I was so depleted that I didn't have anything left in me for things that genuinely mattered.

Something had short-circuited in me. Something was so burned out that the emotions reached a charred dead end before getting to me.

The test results reassured me that my brain wasn't broken in one way—but I couldn't celebrate, because my brain had been broken in another.

I did my best to go through the motions. I celebrated my negative results by buying myself the doll I'd always wanted as a child. I took a wood crafting class and came home with a handmade blanket rack. I finished my last week of classes and looked over my take-home final. I fished out the overnight backpack that I'd never used and prepared for my first overnight hike. I decided it was time to truly set my sights forward—and away from the past. I'd already been robbed of one meaningful moment. It was time to invest back in myself.

But once again, the second I tried to stand up and walk away was the second something big fell into my lap. But it felt like an anvil had been dropped.

"The girl reached out to me," Danielle texted.

My stomach dropped.

The seventeen-year-old girl—who had grown into a young twentysomething. We finally had a name and a face to the stories.

"She saw my post," Danielle continued. "I'm going to see if she's willing to talk a little more with me."

I agreed with the plan. I tried to refocus. I tried to return to the final exam that I'd started before I'd gotten sidetracked by Danielle's text. I did my best to give the exam every ounce of my attention.

THE YEAR OF DATING MYSELF

"She was willing to talk to me," Danielle texted again, a little while later. I immediately abandoned my final and picked up my phone. "Do you want to know the details?"

I took a hard swallow.

"Yes. I want to know," I replied, the words on my screen not looking like my own.

I tried to prepare myself, but there's no such thing in moments like that.

Danielle relayed what the young woman had been through: how the high schooler had won the lead role in an independent production that he was directing. He'd made her believe that they were in love. He'd drive to her house after midnight, help her sneak out of her parents' house, and take her to a hotel room. She didn't understand it, back then. She just thought she was special, having this older man—a *director* no less—be interested in her. Be her *boyfriend*, albeit a secret one. It wasn't until she entered her twenties that she realized the truth.

She wanted to say something. She wanted to call him out but feared getting sued. She feared the very thing that he threatened me and Britt with.

I gripped my phone.

"Christ. Christ almighty," was my reply.

I walked away from my desk. There was no way I was finishing my exam that day.

I once thought I knew what the feeling was, the space past rage. I thought I knew. And maybe I did. If that were the case, then there's a feeling past *that*, one that taps into something dark.

It was so much worse than I anticipated. My stomach churned, thinking of him driving to her parents' house at night. I imagined him checking into the hotel—good Lord, did he have her wait in the car? Did he sneak her around back?

The monster.

I cried hot, relentless, rageful tears. I talked with Danielle about it, with Britt, with Stella, with Lana, and with Lindsey. I told them that there was no fear left in me. I gave Danielle permission to send the young woman my contact information. I told Danielle that I would help her in any way that I could.

"The big sisters are protecting the little sisters now," I said, and started crying again. I thought of how protective I'd become of the young woman—the *child*, good Lord a twenty-two-year-old is still a *child*—and I flashed white with blinding fury.

I saw someone to protect. He'd seen something to exploit.

The *fucking* monster.

I cried for the rest of the day—and as the day turned into night. I cried from the anger and disgust. I cried for every girl who had a similar story of an older man in a position of power doing something like that to them. I cried because of how *common* that scenario is.

And I cried for myself.

When you leave an abusive relationship, you become obsessed with the truth. You do whatever you can to learn about what really happened when your back was turned—and who your ex-partner *really* was.

But what's that saying again? "Be careful what you wish for."

I had asked for the truth, but I had no idea what I was asking for. I had no idea what I'd tapped into. I'd been on the hunt for answers, and then forced to deal with what the hunt brought in.

Something inside you breaks when you realize the kind of person you'd inadvertently invited into your life. It's like learning that your neighbor was a serial killer—or that a demon had been lurking in the shadows of your house for years.

How do you trust, after something like that? When the person you once held the closest to your heart turns out to be the worst of humanity, what's left for you to do?

THE YEAR OF DATING MYSELF

I had arrived at the truth. It sat squarely at the gates of hell and dared me to come closer to it.

What else was there to do now but burst into a ball of flames? Abandon all hope, ye who enter.

Chapter 31: Timing, Pacing

I waited for her call.

The young woman told Danielle that she was going to reach out to me to talk to me about everything.

Silence.

I tried to recenter myself. I finished my exam. I handed in my final paper. I took scalding hot showers.

I tried to refocus.

I prepared for my first overnight hike. I went into the woods behind my house and practiced setting up camp.

I sat in discomfort. All that rage, and nowhere for it to go. I told Danielle I was spiraling, and Danielle disagreed.

"You're not spiraling," she said. "You're the shark in the water, circling its target."

I was the shark. I felt inhuman. I felt primal.

I felt like a grizzly bear mama. I was ready to cause carnage. I was ready to protect at all costs.

She was a *child*. She was *still* a child.

The fucking *monster*.

I refrained from reaching out. I knew my energy was aggressive— and I knew how unhelpful that energy was. Even benevolent aggressive energy could cause harm. I knew, because I knew how *I* had responded in the past, to "benevolent" aggression. I had to trust in the timing of all things. It had been downright divine before. Why doubt it then?

In that waiting, a voice inside me began its refrain.

"*Are you trying to save her to make up for the fact that you couldn't save yourself?*"

The question turned me from a mama grizzly bear into a baby black bear, scampering up the tree in terror. It broke me from being the circling shark and forced me to be the human treading water.

I saw so much of myself in her, and it was not just because we shared an abuser.

I never saw justice for any of the things that happened to me in the past. I never saw justice for any of the men who had violated my body, who stole my innocence (or stole what little remained of it).

I couldn't balance my own scales. Would balancing the scales for others make up for it?

Does anything make up for a lack of retribution?

I had no answers. But I did have a reservation for a pottery class, and I forced myself to go.

That man had taken so much. He wasn't about to take away my date night.

I'd never done pottery before, and it became clear during the class that, unlike ax throwing, I would *not* get the hang of it by the end of class.

I tried to make a bowl, only to watch the sides wobble out.

"Ah, I see what's happening," said the instructor. "You're moving your hands too fast up the sides."

I looked down at my bowl, which had taken on a spiral shape.

"I mean, usually, that's not a bad speed for your hands," the instructor continued, "but your clay wheel is currently going too slow for it, so you have to slow down your movements."

I thanked her, dipped my hands in my water, and tried again.

The metaphor was louder than any voice in the room. Sometimes a productive speed is not the universal speed. The right pace will depend entirely on the circumstances. Sometimes everything around you is going slower, and the only thing you can do is slow down as well.

Attempting what *should've* been a proper speed won't give you the results you want. When the world around you is applying the brakes, you must do the same.

Life is poetry, complete with iambic beats.

I filmed myself making another bowl, excited to make a time lapse of my creation. I watched the video the next day, and felt something in me break.

The footage was completely unusable. Not because of the lighting or the angles. It was because I looked like I was on the verge of tears the entire time.

In concentrating on the clay, I had dropped all pretense. I had stopped contorting my face into a permanent grin, the joker's smile of people pleasers everywhere. Underneath that contortion was someone whose sorrow emanated.

No wonder no one really talked to me at the pottery class.

Chapter 32: Return

"He's back," Stella messaged me on the morning of my hike. I felt my stomach drop.

"He's refusing to acknowledge that he threatened to sue you," Danielle said. "That won't fly with me. I'm going to make some noise."

I took a breath. I bit my tongue.

"We missed you!" "Welcome back!" So many of the comments, all from *women*, heralded his return. I kept repeating to myself that it was a good thing I'd be disappearing into the wilderness for forty-eight hours, away from cell signal.

Away from all of it.

"How are you faring?" Danielle asked.

I tried to answer as succinctly as I could.

I felt powerless. Society was designed to prop up men and look past their indiscretions—and no matter what sins of a man are exposed, there will always be enough women who will vie for his attention. Even the most brutal serial killers get fan mail in prison, after all.

"I can't stop thinking *society protects men like him, and sometimes there's no justice*," I replied to Danielle.

THE YEAR OF DATING MYSELF

I knew some of those women who'd heralded his return had also been ones to call me a liar and a bitch. I knew some had seen the evidence against him and still contended that he was good and I must be evil. I had to wonder if these women were so eager to tear down a woman in honor of a man because the alternative was unbearable.

To defend the system is to be given a promise that you'll be spared. But to be in defiance is to see how unjust it all is. To disobey a world that taught you to hate yourself and hate your gender is to realize how much that world had taught you to hate yourself and hate your gender; that following the rules never actually gave you the reward it promised.

That for all your defense of the system, you'll never be spared from it.

And—most times—there will be no justice.

I packed up my car and hit the road for the trailhead. A part of me was anxious that I'd be in the woods, with no way to check in with friends, or even call for help. Another part was grateful. I needed to disconnect. I needed to get away from it.

I'm so tired. I don't want to do this anymore.

Somehow, my Year of Dating Myself went from self-love while echoes of my past danced in my ears, to looking directly at the cause and hearing it scream.

A line had been crossed. A threshold had been met. Something in me had broken.

I needed to get *away.*

It was a bittersweet relief when I got to the trailhead and found not an iota of cell service. I dragged out my pack and sighed at its heftiness.

I was reminded of Cheryl Strayed's memoir *Wild*, particularly her overstuffed pack—lovingly named Monster. I'd read her memoir soon after my father died, when my marriage was on the rocks and I didn't understand why I was so messed up. I saw so much of my plight in hers. I was hoping for immediate answers, because that's what you do when you're at a complicated crossroads: you want quick answers and clear-cut solutions.

How frustrated I was when I finished the memoir without either.

I shrugged on my pack. I took off on my trail at a gentle clip. I was deliberately taking an unpopular set of trails that went up zero mountains—but it did follow a beautiful sandstone river to a remote waterfall. It was my hope to savor the trails, not just charge through them, like I had so many times in the past.

I said hello to the few hikers I passed, who were heading back to the trailhead. After I passed a tent site, I stopped passing hikers.

Alone on the trails, I started thinking about things. I broiled in my fury as I thought about what my ex had put me through. I thought about the young woman, and what he'd done to her.

I was sweating and hyperventilating when I realized I'd been speed walking.

Hikes were always where I perseverated. The trails gave me permission to broil. It was a familiar feeling. I'd circled the same topic until something finally softened.

"How often I give my rage as an offering to Mother Nature," I said aloud.

I continued my trek. I was behind schedule, even with the speed walking. I'd grossly miscalculated, and the mileage was far more than I was anticipating. The trails were becoming more rugged and less maintained. One trail was completely washed out in a few spots and I had to trek down to the river to get around it.

Eventually a memory returned to me: one from the summer after my father died.

Lana had just moved to the area, a few years after Samuel had passed away. Her new partner—the man she'd go on to

THE YEAR OF DATING MYSELF

marry—wanted to take us on a hike: a trail that ran a parallel path, but on the opposite side of the river.

Lana and I opened up during that hike in ways that we hadn't before. I talked about my father; she talked about hers. We talked about our lives with a depth that we hadn't yet traversed.

There's something about the trails that brings out the rawness in our souls.

How often we offer our most authentic selves as an offering to Mother Nature.

I thought about that memory as I scrambled up another riverbank. My legs were shaking by the time I got to the rock ledge right by the waterfall, a loud and powerful force that curved its way down hundreds of feet of cliffside.

I was exhausted. My boots were waterlogged. But I made it. I was there.

I made it to *my* waterfall.

I took off my boots and gave my feet—which had gone white and wrinkly—a chance to recover. Just past where I put my pack lay five butterflies, all slowly flapping their wings in the sun. One of the butterflies landed on my pack.

I had no choice but to take it as a good omen.

I sat with the waterfall, ate as much as I could, and tried to rest. I checked my phone and found zero cell signal. I knew that if I didn't have any signal there, at arguably the highest point in elevation for my hike, I wouldn't have a signal at any point.

Sometimes sitting in discomfort looks a lot like pressing forward with your original plan.

I eventually got up. I shifted my pack, disrupting the butterfly. I put on new socks and slipped my feet into my wet boots and continued on.

But, once again, I was charging through the trails. It was a combination of fear and disdain: fear, because I risked not getting to my planned camping place in time, and disdain, because the trails turned into a murky, swampy, miserable mess.

I became a miserable mess to match, slogging through the unending miles. I stepped in what I thought was a small puddle and my leg sunk up to my knee.

"Are you *fucking* kidding me?!" I shouted out. I was grateful I was still alone, with only Mother Nature to see me in that state.

I was frustrated with the trails, with myself. I'd spent years suffering through trails at a breakneck pace. My waterfall hike was supposed to be a counterbalance to those years—and yet, there I was, doing more of the same.

Tediously, the miles ticked away, and I finally left the swamp behind. I continued down the path, racing against the setting sun, until I got to the very place I'd hoped to camp for the night.

I breathed a sigh of relief at the river junction. I set up my hammock, tied up my pack, and sat down by the river. I mindlessly shoveled food into my mouth, washing it down with large, messy gulps of water. I had plans for after setting up camp. I wanted to dip in the deeper parts of the river. I had my book to read.

None of it was going to happen.

I did dip into the river, but only for long enough to haphazardly wash the sweat and dirt off my skin. I changed into my nightwear, climbed into my hammock, and stared at the treetops. I felt like Cheryl Strayed again, at that moment. Just like her, the only thing I had left to offer Mother Nature was my exhaustion.

But maybe that's what was so healing about those kinds of excursions. It's not just a return to something primal. It's a stripping away of everything until *all that's left* is the primal.

Sometimes a factory reset comes from short-circuiting yourself, from offering every single thought as an offering to Mother Nature, including the ones you can no longer conjure up.

I desperately wanted to stay awake until sunset, to watch the stars twinkle in the unadulterated sky, but my eyelids drooped before dusk settled. I zipped up my sleeping bag and allowed myself to sleep.

I woke up before dawn could introduce itself. The air was chilly, making my sleeping bag even more welcoming. I got up only to grab my food and bring it into the hammock. I ate and watched the world around me. I reluctantly left my cozy bedside, motivated only by the knowledge that rain was expected in the afternoon.

I closed my campsite with a profound sense of Zen. There was something beautiful in taking a place you called home, even temporarily, and dismantling it until it fit into a bag. It was a reminder of how transient it all is. Our houses and apartments are made of concrete and wood, but all of it will be dismantled in the end too.

I returned to the main trail that would bring me back to my car. Aside from a slip on a rock that scraped up my knee, the rest of the hike was uneventful. I strolled where I could. I enjoyed the views that I'd appreciated the day before, but from the opposite direction, and with storm clouds rolling in. I passed the tent site again, which had become completely vacant. I wondered if I'd go a full twenty-four hours without seeing anyone, only to see a trail runner at the twenty-third hour. I returned to the trailhead, got in my car, and started driving back toward the highway.

I returned home in awe of how normal everything felt, like I was just picking up where I left off. The world around me was the same, yet something in me was different.

There was a grit that hadn't been there before. A grit that replaced my apprehension about camping overnight in the remote wilderness. A grit that softened a few of my jagged edges.

But there was also exhaustion. After a proper shower and meal, I laid down in bed for a nap, only to fall into a deep sleep for seven hours. I awoke to the sun which had long since set, got up for another meal, and then fell asleep for another seven hours.

After months of disrupted sleep, it had been a godsend. Not including COVID, I couldn't remember the last time I'd slept so soundly.

Sometimes a factory reset can only come when you've drained the batteries dry.

Chapter 33: Blended

Three days after my hike, I returned to the mountains in a vintage dress. I had a table for one on an old-timey dinner train, one that slowly made its way through the White Mountains.

I checked in at the station platform, doing my best to stand tall while standing amongst a sea of couples. I could feel a few eyes on me. A past version of me would've wilted under the scrutiny, making myself small, my body language apologizing for daring to take up space.

I instead held my head up a little higher than before.

Gentle jazz music played through the speakers as I boarded the train. I walked past a wall of posters from the 1950s, with old-fashioned luggage delicately stacked on its shelves. The jazz music brought me back to Sunday mornings as a child, getting ready for church as my father's radio played—one of those pure childhood memories, the kind you hold delicately with one hand and hold back the darker memories with the other.

I enjoyed my five-course meal and watched the train roll past the same rivers that I'd waded through, just a few days earlier and just a little farther north. I relished being alone at my table. I could just watch the scenery. I didn't have to keep conversation with the person sitting across from me. I didn't have to worry if the person across the table was having a good time.

I didn't have to wonder if the person across the table was secretly a monster.

The train eventually retraced its steps back to the station. I sipped on my coffee, trying to remember the last time I'd eaten that well. As we returned to the platform, I'd decided that the reason I kept getting looks was not because I was a loner, a weirdo sticking out like a sore thumb—it was because they all assumed I was someone important.

Who was this woman, dolled up and by herself, boarding this train? Is she a food critic? A travel writer? A celebrity?!

Who is this woman standing defiantly on her own?

I finally got to see my therapist later that week.

The last time I'd seen her was when the first cease and desist email had landed in my inbox. There was a lot to catch her up on. I told her about the young woman. I told her about feeling a type of mama bear protection, and about feeling nothing when I got my negative Alzheimer's test.

"What part, do you think, is running the show right now?" she asked.

I was stumped. At that point, I'd become proficient at navigating the different parts of me. I knew when "Wounded Child Abby" was calling the shots. I knew when "Logical Abby" was running the show and when "Emotional Abby" was getting her chance to breathe.

But that? I had no answer.

"I mean, it's not my wounded child side, at least I don't think," I said. "It's not logical me, because there's too much rage—but I don't think it's teen me. It's also not Emotional Abby, because, well, there are a lot of emotions that I'm not feeling right now."

I still wondered how I would've taken the news about the Alzheimer's test, had circumstances been different.

"It's not my higher self. At least I don't think. But there are elements of her there," I paused. "There are elements of a lot of parts."

My therapist grinned.

"From what I'm observing, we might have a brand-new part," she said. "One that is a blend of other parts—the best of those parts."

I paused again.

"I think you're right."

"This is a good thing," she explained. "It's a sign that your parts are becoming a little less compartmentalized. They're starting to work together. It's no longer about competition to steer the ship."

I nodded.

"This new part is coming from necessity, yes, but it's a cooperative response," she said. "This is a sign of healing."

I could only grin sheepishly.

We scheduled our next appointment. Between her schedule and mine, I wouldn't see her again until after my birthday, which was in September and less than a month away.

"I'll try not to have a lifetime's worth of events to recall, next time," I joked.

I drove home, trying to absorb what my therapist had said.

The parts of me were blending. I was put under extreme stress and what emerged was a collaboration. Something that could hold space for rage, yet hold back from acting on it.

But I was having a hard time believing that it was a sign of healing.

Maybe it's because of what *wasn't* said in my therapist's office. What I didn't tell her—what I hadn't told anyone: that my drinking

THE YEAR OF DATING MYSELF

had skyrocketed. I was polishing off a bottle of wine in a single evening, without even getting a buzz.

I knew *why* it happened. I was on edge constantly. I still held my breath every time I checked my email. Going online felt like having a live bomb in my hands. I'd bought a doorbell with a security camera attached to it—and then bought two more cameras. Survival mode gives the world a laser-sharp focus, and the edges of everything become too painful to look at.

I wanted to soften the edges.

I wanted softness.

I wanted my shoulders to relax away from my ears.

I wanted to rest my racing heart.

I wanted to rest.

I'm so tired. I don't want to do this anymore.

Part IX:
September

Chapter 34: Taking Care

"Those flowers better be for you!" The cashier exclaimed as they scanned the bouquet and gave me a mischievous look.

"They are, actually," I beamed. It had become a ritual of mine; buying myself flowers every time I shopped at the grocery store.

"That's so important," the cashier responded. "Y'know, to be kind to yourself like that!"

"I completely agree," I said. "It's been my focus as of late."

"Oh, I love that. Too many people just don't know how to love themselves. I bet you have some great mentors . . ."

My facial expression must've signaled otherwise.

". . . or you've gone through some great adversity," the cashier shifted, "to be in this place."

"Definitely door number two," I replied self-consciously, adding, "I didn't really love myself, and there are a lot of people who are happy to take advantage of that."

"Well, you're doing it now, and that's what matters!"

I paid for my items and wished the cashier a good day. Our brief conversation was a reassurance, a reminder that I was on the right path.

THE YEAR OF DATING MYSELF

My fall semester had just begun. Despite abandoning the final exam halfway through, I somehow made it out with an A for my summer class. Another semester with my 4.0 GPA intact; but barely. I was doing terribly on my promise to focus more on school during my Year of Dating Myself.

One of my fall classes required weekly documentation of self-care practices. In my first entry, I wrote in vague terms about dating myself. I wrote about some of the more stereotypical self-care from the week: a nature walk, morning cardio, the flowers . . .

But the more important self-care activities didn't make the journal entry.

I didn't talk about registering my car on the first of the month, like a healing tribute to the version of me who got pulled over in February for her expired registration and invalid plates. I didn't talk about visiting a dispensary because I needed *something* to curb my drinking.

And I didn't talk about the decision to put down my sword and shield. I'd been prepared for war ever since the young woman reached out to Danielle. I was ready to show the young woman that it wasn't a fight that she had to do alone.

She'd reached out to Danielle again. In her message, she told Danielle that she was ready to share her story with the world—she just wished she knew what to say to me. Danielle replied, offering to have me reach out, to let me take on the mantle of starting the conversation.

Danielle's message sat unopened.

I didn't talk about how self-care sometimes looks like recognizing that it is not your boat to steer. I had to be honest with myself about what was motivating me. I knew that if I imposed my timeline, I'd be doing something *regardless* of what was best for her, not *because* of it.

Sometimes self-care is understanding why you had a death grip on your sword and shield in the first place.

I didn't talk about how I could feel a chapter closing—and how it *needed* to close. For the first time in almost a year, I didn't want to keep going until the chapter had a happy ending.

Sometimes self-care is knowing when to set down the mantle.

I did end my journal entry for school with: *Admittedly, self-care sometimes looks like giving yourself grace when you need to rest.*

Which, in some ways, was a neat summary of what I didn't say.

I got a message from my younger brother on Labor Day that our Great Aunt Peggy had passed away. She'd been my mother's aunt; my grandmother's sister.

My heart sank. While I'd only met her in person once, I'd been thinking about her a lot. Among my childhood toys, I'd found one of her educational kits, unopened. A crystal growing kit, potentially the last kit she'd sent me.

I would've been seventeen.

I'd been planning to do the kit, partly as a solo date, and partly as a type of communion with that younger side of me, the one who spent hours engrossed in her annual, kid-friendly experiments. I'd also been searching for the whereabouts of my Great Aunt Peggy.

I didn't know what state she lived in. I didn't even know her last name. As I had scoured for clues, I realized how little I knew about *anything* involving my mother's side of the family.

Gabe, who'd been helping in the research, had verbalized what I was longing for:

"It'd be nice to connect with a family member you have fond memories of."

THE YEAR OF DATING MYSELF

Aunt Peggy never had children. My mother was her next of kin. My brother, who had power of attorney, was effectively in charge of settling the estate. I did my best to help, researching estate lawyers and funeral homes, coordinating a burial in Vermont for someone who'd died in California. At least I knew her whereabouts, albeit far too late.

"I'm in a weird headspace," I mumbled to myself. I mumbled it again as I grabbed the crystal kit from my desk.

It wasn't until after I finished the experiment, when I was splashing water on my tear-blotched face, that I found the words for my emotions: I was grieving the hypothetical.

My father's side was robust—but what little good that was, since I'd effectively cut off contact with them. My mother, an only child, was cognitively as good as gone. My maternal grandparents were long dead, and the one remaining relative that could've been my tie back to my roots had just passed away.

I ached for the ability to talk to Aunt Peggy—as well as my maternal grandmother. I wanted to know about their lives. I wanted to know of the worlds that existed long before I was born, before even my mother was born. I'd learned a few years back that my grandmother had hated my father. *Hated* him. She wanted my mom to leave him. She practically demanded it. My grandmother told my mom that if my mom didn't divorce my father, she would change her will so that her estate would skip my mom entirely and be given to my brother and myself.

Dementia robbed my grandmother of her mind before she could make good on that threat.

That information had stuck with me, but there was one detail that I hadn't paid attention to, until the day I learned Aunt Peggy had died: the threat to write my mother out of her will was not made early on in their relationship. The revised benefactors were going to be my brother and myself—which meant my parents had been married for years by that point.

It meant my grandmother had witnessed the destruction. She wasn't just upset that her daughter was with someone she didn't approve of.

She knew what was happening at home. And she knew it wasn't okay.

I thought about Aunt Peggy. Her devotion to her grand niece and nephew. The Christmas gifts that arrived every year, without fail.

What did she know about our situation? How close were she and my grandma?

Did my grandma tell her about my father? Did my mom tell her?

I'd spent my adult life clinging to men because I would've given anything for a sense of family. I'd hand over my power because I wanted to know what it felt like to be cared for. I'd spent my adult life scrambling for a sense of home because home had never been a safe place as a child.

When I was old enough to realize healthy families didn't operate like mine, I was overwhelmed with betrayal. Was no other adult paying attention? Did no one try to do anything?

But as an adult, I better understand the powerlessness of the person outside of the situation. What more can be done, outside of persuasion, or demands, or even ultimatums?

What more can be done, other than educational gifts at Christmas, sent from across the country, with love?

Chapter 35: An Itch You Can't Scratch

I sat in the physical therapy clinic at my university, biting my tongue. It had nothing to do with the pain I'd been dealing with—a constant tug in my neck, something that had been gradually getting worse until I felt the tension up the left side of my face.

As the doctoral candidate moved my head around, I realized just how touch starved I was. And the realization pinged loudly within me.

I calculated how much touch I got in any given week. I saw Lana every week or two—which usually meant a hug hello and a hug goodbye.

And that . . . was the end of the list.

I hadn't seen a massage therapist in months, not after one session sent ripples of pain from the tense spot on my neck. Facials—outside of promotional coupons—were too expensive. The PT student's examination was the first time another human had touched me in weeks. It was a sobering moment. I was investing in a platonic community, but most of its members were scattered across the country. I had my solo dates, but touching my own arm was not the same as when someone else did it.

I had to contend with the contradiction: I was surrounded by people I loved, but I was also isolated. There was an ache for something, and I wasn't sure what it was. All I knew is that I couldn't scratch the itch myself, no matter how hard I tried.

I didn't ask anyone at the drug rehab facility. I figured it out on my own.

I hadn't seen the handsome clinician with the kind eyes in weeks. The door to his office was closed and quiet. A smattering of new, temporary faces filled the nurse's station.

Turnover rates were notoriously high at the facility. He'd only been working there since March, but I'd yet to see any kind-eyed employee last longer than a year. It was the more grizzled individuals—the drug counselors who'd also been in the trenches, the nurses who'd cut their teeth on emergency room night shifts—who stayed for longer. It was a tough and taxing environment. I was shielded from most of it as a group facilitator who was only there for an hour or two a day.

There was no sadness in realizing he was gone. There was no longing.

There was *relief*.

There was a sense of finality—and, in that finality, the relief intensified. It felt like coming home to find out someone had cleared out the alcohol. It was in that relief that I realized how protective I'd become of my emotional sobriety. I thought of all the times where infatuation had led to destruction. I thought of the men who'd weaponized that infatuation, the men who benefited from it without any reciprocation.

Part of my ache during physical therapy was a withdrawal symptom. I knew that much. I missed the high of complete enrapture in another person. But, like anyone in withdrawal from what had been destroying their life, the last thing I needed was to get another fix.

In my second self-care entry for class, I talked about using the plastic water slide.

I made use of the hot weather—the reminder that summer had no interest in giving over to autumn—and hooked up the slide to the garden hose. I brought Salem out with me, letting him explore the front yard on his leash as I slid down the plastic runway until my skin ached from the cold water.

As I toweled myself off and hung the slide to dry, I thought about how my Year of Dating Myself had also been a year of parenting myself. It had been the first year I'd been able to really hold that wounded child side of me close and be the parent she needed.

The year was also an apology tour, in some ways: I had kept putting her in harm's way with the men I'd been dating, and it didn't matter that I understood, logically, that it was that very wounded child side that had attached to men who were like my father. I still thought of how I cried, the night before my last birthday, on a video call with my then-boyfriend, devastated at the antics he was pulling to avoid being with me on the day. I cried the way a child who'd been told her birthday party was canceled would cry.

I was effectively a single mom, learning to make it on her own, and making it up to her child.

It was why my Year of Dating Myself *had* to include something special for my birthday. I was only a few weeks away from it. Lana was helping me make reservations and come up with ideas. Several women from the online community were flying in for it. Others were driving in. Everyone agreed that the weekend would be a triumph over abuse. I'd tried to devote my previous birthday weekend to a man who didn't love me; that year my friends were enthusiastically devoting my birthday weekend to *me*.

In many ways, the Year of Dating Myself was not just an apology tour to my wounded child side, but to *myself*. My Solo Tour was a chance to say the one thing I wished so many exes would've said, but never did: "I'm sorry for what I put you through. Let me make it up to you."

The day of the comedy show—the one I'd bought my box seat for—rushed to my feet. September had felt so far away when I'd purchased my ticket, but suddenly it was the day of the event.

It made sense. My summer had blazed past me. My sense of time had burned with it. Only in September did it feel like things were starting to reduce to embers.

I drove into Boston and walked to the theater. A part of me had been worried about being the lone seat in a row of three. I worried about the awkwardness, how glaring it would be that I was *alone*.

But I realized something, as the rest of the box filled up, as the show started: No one cared.

The couple who shared the row with me sat down with barely a hello. There was nary a glance or a questioning stare in my direction.

No one cared that I was *by myself*.

There was something liberating in that realization. People, by and large, are too wrapped up in their own worlds to care about yours. Any worry that an endeavor will be met with scrutiny is usually unfounded. Most of the time, they won't even register that you're there.

But I had another realization that night. The echoes of my touch starvation still lingered, tugging at me as incessantly as the tension in my neck. The couple in the row in front of me spent the entire show enveloped in each other. They cuddled and canoodled. The display of affection was constant.

It repulsed me.

I wasn't repulsed at *them*, per se—but their affection was like being presented with spoiled food. I wanted none of it, no matter how hungry I was.

I didn't know what to make of the realization. In some ways, it was reassuring: the stirring, the starvation, wouldn't be quelled by a romantic embrace. The ache, at the end of the day, posed no threat to my Solo Tour.

But there was something maddening about desperately wanting something in theory, but not in practice. I yearned to lean against a beloved, to rest my head on their shoulder, but I was also disgusted by it. I'd studied enough trauma psychology to know how inevitable such a disorganized desire was. But it didn't change how disorienting it felt.

It also did nothing to quiet the voice that said that I was past the point of no return—that I would never be "fit" for a romantic relationship again . . .

. . . if I'd ever been fit for one in the first place.

Chapter 36: Pop Quiz

A week before my birthday, I got my first haircut in over a year—and that was on purpose. I had to deliberately grow my hair out to see if cutting off most of it had actually been for me.

I once had incredibly long hair. But during my previous relationship, I'd chopped it off, my hair just inches away from my jaw. I thought it was something I'd done on my own volition (and, coincidentally, how *lucky* I was to have a boyfriend who just so happened to prefer *that haircut* on *women*?!).

In the aftermath of that relationship, I'd learned that it was a well-established pattern that the women he dated all inevitably got that haircut, and usually within the last months of the relationship. When people from his local community reached out, I'd learn that some had been keeping tabs on me. When they saw that I'd cut off my hair, they knew that the relationship was done for.

Hearing that had rattled me. Was that decision yet another extension of his manipulation? I genuinely wanted to believe otherwise, but there was only one way for me to know.

It was reassuring, as my hair grew back, that I itched to have it short again. Perhaps I'd never fully know if my original decision had been 100 percent my own. But what mattered was that in the present day, it was what I wanted. However, it wasn't until I got home that I realized the severe asymmetry to my cut. One side had fun, dynamic, shaggy layers. The other side was a straight bob.

In the past, I would've told myself that I could deal with it.

This is a pop quiz on how much progress you've made in your healing, I told myself as I called the salon and asked if I could get it fixed. The salon was warm and responsive, and the stylist was happy to balance everything out.

Sometimes it's a triumphant act of defiance to be willing to take up space with your wants.

A few days after my touch up, I had a video call with my friend Toni. She was looking to move from Wyoming to Oregon, but nothing was really coming to fruition. Her realtor in Oregon was researching properties, traveling to them on Toni's behalf, and then going back to the drawing board when things fell through. Toni was grappling with the guilt of "making" her realtor do all that work.

"I'm reminding myself that this is her job," said Toni. "She makes money by finding me a house."

"We're conditioned to apologize for our very existence," I said. "We're told we should never be inconvenient, even in situations where people are getting paid for it. So, we try to be as convenient as possible. Shoot, we'll try to do *their* jobs *for them* because we feel bad that they have to do their jobs for us."

It was becoming clear that we were in a new stage in our healing. We had clawed our way up to what was essentially ground level for others. But it was time to see if we could stand ten toes down on that pavement, even when the slightest breeze made us want to retreat into the trenches.

Something gets wounded in you—a tender spot poked and a raw nerve hit—when someone you love rips your birthday out from under you. So many of us shut down about celebrating birthdays because it leaves us too vulnerable. It's better to not care than to risk exposing ourselves to such a direct way of being told we're not special. With Lana's help, my birthday plans came together. Most were the things that I'd planned to do the previous year, with my then-boyfriend. I was going to go to the Museum of Fine Arts, my old alma mater, and the Prudential Tower's observation deck.

I still needed that corrective experience—and a part of me felt like I'd failed myself in still needing it. But something clicked for me, on the Saturday of my birthday weekend, when my friends and I arrived at the Museum of Fine Arts, which sat just across the street from my alma mater. I stared in wonder at my school, telling my friends how I used to go into the MFA all the time as an under-graduate student, my college ID granting me free access.

Maybe it's not always about returning to the scene of the crime. Sometimes you're returning to your previous context to compare who you were then with who you are now. Sometimes it's more about realizing you've come so far since the last time you were there.

. . . That was what I repeated to myself as I took measured breaths, watching my plans for the day fall apart.

Getting into Boston had taken hours. I'd timidly reminded the friends who were staying at my house that we needed to go, that we were already behind schedule, but my meek reminders had no impact. The delay had a domino effect. The original plan of explor-ing the museum before lunch turned into tracking down friends who'd disappeared to buy lunch at the museum's cafeteria. I scrapped my plans to walk through my old college campus, desperate to get to the observation deck in time.

THE YEAR OF DATING MYSELF

I took more measured breaths as one friend asked to stop at the reflection pool by the Prudential Tower so they could take a few selfies. The request produced another domino effect. As the women took selfies and requested others to take their photos, I stood off to the side, longingly looking up at the tower.

"The winds are really high right now," I told myself. "They probably have the observation deck closed, anyway."

Canceling the campus visit had not fixed the schedule. If we had walked directly to the ticket kiosk at the ground floor of the Prudential Tower, we would've had, at best, thirty minutes. The selfie stop meant canceling it altogether.

"This is just a lesson in slowing down," I told myself. "I shouldn't have made such a jam-packed schedule. It's okay."

I stifled the loneliness that washed over me, the feeling of being the fifth wheel on my own birthday. I could hear my ex's voice in my head.

You need constant attention. I can't have a single moment to myself. It's gotta be about you, 24/7. Fuck me and what I need, right?

"It doesn't need to be about me, 24/7," I told myself. "Look at the people who traveled to see me. Some of them have never been to Boston before. They want to enjoy themselves. It's okay. I don't have to be so selfish."

I focused on the dinner at the restaurant Lana had made a reservation for. I focused on the "Happy Birthday" song as the cake came out—a cake Lana had made, just like the year before. I focused on the karaoke after dinner, and how much fun it was to take the mic and belt out a song considering my younger self was too shy to even hum in front of others.

On Sunday morning, the day of my birthday, I focused on how Danielle made breakfast for those who'd slept in after realizing I was going to have to cancel brunch. I reminded myself that the out-of-town friends had done me a solid by spending all that money to come out to see me, so why quibble on the details? I'd already had a dinner—and was going to have a "birthday day" dinner that night—clearly, I was being a diva for wanting to do *brunch* on top of all that.

But the first crack in the foundation formed when we did go out to dinner, that night. While it was a smaller group of people that night, the energy felt even less like my birthday and more like I could've disappeared and no one would've noticed.

It doesn't have to be about me, 24/7, I reminded myself.

The waiter came out with a birthday crème brûlée, the restaurant's traditional treat for the birthday person. I grabbed my spoon as the waiter placed it in front of me. The conversation around me barely paused—and I reminded myself how awkward those "Happy Birthday" serenades were, anyway. Plus, I'd gotten one on Saturday! How *needy* to expect another one!

With my spoon poised over my dessert, I watched another spoon come into my periphery. A spoon that broke into the crème brûlée and grabbed a scoop. The horror I felt must've showed up on my face because I suddenly heard:

"Oh! Have you had any yet?"

I bit my tongue. Obviously, I hadn't. I looked over and noticed that the dessert the friend had ordered for herself hadn't even been touched.

"Oh, I mean, not *yet*," I managed to say, my voice quiet.

"Take my spoon, then! This is yours!" she said, and I placed my spoon down. The new spoon had barely reached my mouth when I watched two people bypass their desserts as well to take from mine. I swallowed quickly and took a few more frantic bites, watching my dessert get eaten in front of me.

It's okay, it's okay, I told myself. *I'm being high maintenance. I'm being too sensitive. It's fine. Look at all these friends who came*

THE YEAR OF DATING MYSELF

out for me! Look at how they took time out of their schedule to spend the whole weekend with me!

I woke up early on Monday to drop some of the ladies off at the airport. My GPS diverted me off the highway, sending me on a wild goose chase through backroads, the highway not even an option on the map. I drove back from the airport, grateful that everyone still got to their flights on time.

I focused on that gratitude. I focused on how the southbound side of the highway was completely closed. Miles and miles of empty highway, followed by miles and miles of parking lot traffic, as four lanes diverted off one exit ramp. There'd been a major crash that morning, barely fifteen minutes before we'd gotten on the road. Had we started our drive to the airport any earlier, we would've been stuck on the highway; had we started our drive any later, and we would've dealt with the backroads becoming jammed as well.

"Look! Just like my flight to Vegas! Everything had to go right in light of everything else going wrong! Things don't have to go according to plan for it to work out!"

It was just like my birthday, *right?* Things don't have to go according to plan! It still worked out!

Wasn't it *so* much better than last year?

It was healing!

Right??

I returned home, feeling the echo of a suddenly empty house. I crawled into bed, pulled the covers over me, and checked the messages on my phone.

My heart stopped as I saw a familiar name.

"Hey, I've been meaning to reach out for a while," read the message from the young woman who was once a seventeen-year-old girl. "It's just been really overwhelming. It's bringing back a lot. But I'd love to still talk with you, if you're still up for it."

Chapter 37: Shattered

"So, how have things been since we last met?"

I saw my therapist a few days after my birthday. I plastered a big smile on my face as I talked about the weekend. I told her about scrapping plans (but that was *on me* for making the weekend so jam-packed! Wasn't it amazing that I could be so flexible?), and about how *healing* it was to have a big birthday celebration.

"Hmm," My therapist tilted her chin. "And how is Emotional Abby doing?"

"Oh, she's doing great!" I replied. "I mean, I was able to have a great, connecting time with my friends!"

My therapist readjusted in her seat, her sign that she'd just caught something.

"This is very interesting. Usually, when I ask about Emotional Abby, she comes out easily. But today? I asked how Emotional Abby was doing, and Logic Abby answered for her."

I bit my tongue. Another crack in the foundation formed, and that one ran across the entire facade.

I started talking about the weekend mishaps that had bothered me. Every time I tried to counter it with reason, my therapist interrupted with: "Logic Abby, go away! This is about emotions only."

THE YEAR OF DATING MYSELF

Multiple times my therapist had to interrupt me with, "Logic Abby, go away!" Each time I was forced to return to my emotions, another crack formed.

I talked about standing in my bedroom, waiting for the ladies to get ready, feeling invisible as the time slipped by. I talked about how it felt like I'd hosted a girls' trip to Boston, despite my friends' declaration that the weekend was about undoing the damage from the previous birthday and making me feel special.

"I know some saw what was happening and tried to help . . ."

"Logic Abby, go away!"

I thought about Sunday morning, and how Danielle made breakfast when I realized we'd never make it to brunch in time. I thought about how the ladies were still in bed as scrambled eggs and English muffins were delivered to them.

"I spent Sunday morning reassuring myself that it was no big deal that we weren't going to my birthday brunch—as others got breakfast in bed," I said—and something in me shattered.

That birthday was supposed to showcase how *different* my life had become. But instead, I'd reverted to the old version of me. I became the wallflower, the meek doormat. I shrugged off plans and desires instead of asserting them because—*God*—who was I to think I ever deserve anything? I'd stifled all my feelings down because I *needed* my birthday to be proof that *I* was worthy of celebrating, that I was more than just an accommodating footnote in someone else's story.

And I'd been an accommodating footnote for my own birthday.

I'd hosted a girls' trip. A trip that was on everyone else's schedule but mine. A trip that prioritized everyone else's needs but my own. A trip where I made myself flexible and small, where I slipped to the sidelines. I knew it was more complicated than that. I knew everyone meant well. I knew Lana had pulled out all the stops with planning and Danielle was trying to help and—

"Logic Abby, go away!"

The foundation completely gave way from under me.

My wounded child side came out in force. She cried like someone had just unwrapped all her presents on her. She cried like someone had not just blown out her birthday candles, but grabbed a chunk of the cake.

Just like my birthday dessert was eaten right from under me.

The parallels were so direct, it was no wonder it hurt so deep.

It was no wonder that "Logic Abby" had built a fortress around her, to reassure everyone that *it was fine* and *I was just being too sensitive.*

I'd defaulted to the same behaviors that kept me in a holding pattern in my previous relationship.

I was barely a week away from the one-year anniversary of when I'd left him, but apparently nothing had changed. The only difference was that I already understood why I'd done it. I'd *needed* a corrective experience for my birthday. And what's worse than watching your friends proclaim that your birthday will be special, your birthday will serve as a triumph, only to then watch your birthday get taken away from you?

I tried to think about how I could make it up to myself, only to collapse further. Why did I have to *make up* for the birthday that was supposed to *make up* for the previous year's?

And what was I going to do when it came to my friends? What was I going to say to them—if anything at all?

I'd been conditioned since childhood to be responsible for everyone else's emotions—and to be punished if I were to show any of my own. It was how my parents operated. It was how my ex operated. I was never *allowed* to be hurt, and I could never perfect

THE YEAR OF DATING MYSELF

my words enough to be spared from the wrath. I'd learned to keep things to myself—or to be prepared to spend more time tending to the person who'd *caused me* harm, usually to the direct exclusion of what had *harmed me* in the first place.

I'd already repeated one old pattern. Would I repeat a second? Forget a pop quiz on my healing; it was the midterm exam.

Chapter 38: Communicate

The young woman and I exchanged a few messages. She told me that she wanted to speak on the phone, and that she'd let me know when she could. I told her that she'd already shown bravery and strength just for talking with Danielle.

"He's such a master manipulator. It makes me want to go over every lie he'd ever said to me," the young woman said, "But that's a fucked-up way of healing."

"There's nothing fucked up about it," I replied. "I'd gone over my entire relationship with him in my head, from start to finish, trying to get to the bottom of every lie. It hurt like hell, but I also knew I needed it."

She promised again that she'd call soon after, but things went quiet after that.

I thought about my mama bear rage from the month before. The slightest hint at the word, "go," would've had me charging. But I had to contend with how much I'd been motivated by my own pain. I had to burn through that rage and that readiness to fight.

In the ashes, was something a lot quieter.

I was there to be what *she* needed. And if all I was needed for—if all I could do—was validate her experience, then I was happy to step into that role.

I slowly started to talk about my birthday.

I started with Lana and Danielle, the friends who'd been the helpers; the ones trying to mitigate. Those conversations were easy enough; their responses were commiserative instead of confrontative. I told them my fears about saying anything to the others—because I knew airplane tickets weren't cheap and it cost them a lot to come see me.

"Them spending money to come see you isn't a good enough reason to stay silent," said Danielle.

I started to reach out to those who were innocent bystanders to the entire thing. The conversations were validating. They had seen what was unfolding, and helped remind me that it wasn't just all in my "oversensitive" head.

I wanted to stop there, but I knew I needed to say something to those whose actions had made me feel like my birthday was stolen from me. Healing romantic wounds with platonic love isn't an easy bypass. No matter what avenue of love you're walking down, you will inevitably hit moments that test it.

It felt Herculean, but I summoned up enough strength to say what I needed to say:

"I'm hurt by how my birthday went."

The most important lesson I ever needed to learn was that, with safe people, you're allowed to say you're hurt. With safe people, you won't be dismissed or yelled at. With safe people, the focus won't be redirected, demanding that you tend to *them* for committing the unforgivable sin of communicating your pain.

ABBY ROSMARIN

Unsafe people are the ones who care more about being seen as safe than truly being safe. Safe people want to know how they can stay a safe person in your life.

In that safety, my wounded child side got her moment to feel heard. A part of me worried that, at any moment, I'd hear, "I've been nothing but patient with you, but you just had to keep pressing me!"—only out of a friend's mouth, instead of my ex's.

That moment never happened—and, in the absence of that moment, the echoes of my ex's voice faded away.

I realized, once again, how misguided, "you need to forgive in order to heal," was. Forgiveness won't suddenly douse the fire of anger and pain. That had been a prime example. I'd forgiven all of them from the start. I knew nothing had been done with malice. I knew that group energy is intoxicating; that it creates fissures between the spotlight-grabbing personalities and those who fade into the background. But I still needed to empty the contents from the pressure cooker that had been my stifled feelings.

Everyone heals differently, but this is what I've learned: to be witnessed is to facilitate healing.

I think that's why so many of us will pour out our traumas to a stranger, why we'll destroy ourselves trying to get the person who harmed us to acknowledge what they did.

We're just desperate for our pain to be witnessed.

Self-growth midterm exam, for all intents and purposes: passed.

Chapter 39: Weight

After feverishly searching for a fencing class, I'd found a place that allowed beginners to drop in. The only drawback was that it was two hours away. My original plan was to drive down, but it had been a taxing week. I was still hurt about my birthday. I desperately wanted to have the energy for the drive, to finally take the fencing class that I'd promised to a month prior.

But the energy never came.

There was no way I was going to be able to do the drive, let alone attend a full martial arts class. Instead, I decided to go on the date I'd been pushing off, despite its simplicity: an at-home movie night.

The nights of just watching anything on TV didn't count. There was a difference between dating yourself and just doing things alone. The key was in the intentionality: a deliberateness to the actions. It's the difference between a partner casually tossing you their phone, their eyes not even meeting yours as you add your order for delivery, and having an emotionally present, romantic dinner for two.

The energy is palpably different.

I set up for my movie night, making popcorn and sugar cookies. I turned off the lights, curled into my blanket, and immersed myself in the movie. What I needed in that moment wasn't some grand expansion to prove the resiliency of my human spirit. What I needed was that quiet celebration of my own company—with no one to eat my dessert out from under me.

A few days later, my breath caught as a notification popped up onto my phone.

I was preparing for a trip down to Raleigh, North Carolina. Britt and I had been invited to be interviewed for a series on queer identity. Danielle lived just outside of Raleigh. It was one of those serendipitous moments that makes you wonder if you'd somehow manifested it yourself. I was getting some packing done when my phone buzzed, and the calendar event displayed across my screen read:

Happy anniversary, you beautiful bitch! You've been free a year!!

I didn't remember creating that event on my calendar. Yet, a part of me—most likely the same part that had had enough gumption to walk away in the first place—had made sure to document such an important day.

Exactly one year prior, I'd broken things off with my then-boyfriend.

A year and a day prior, I had stoically said, "I don't have to do this in front of you," and hung up on my abusive boyfriend. One year ago, I'd told him that I was done—and pushed back on his assertion that I was ending things because he was just "too focused on taking care of his family."

The proclamation of being free for a year wasn't exactly true. In some ways, my ex's tendrils had stayed wrapped around me for a while. When his stunts weren't reminding me that I was still in his blast radius, the echoes of the past reminded me that I was still at ground zero for my pain. I'd been consumed with the truth, consumed with justice. It was only recently that I truly felt free of those shackles.

Before that, I'd been the opposite of free—but it had been like staying in the prison until every cell block had been liberated.

Regardless, I'd been single for exactly one year. The last time I'd been single for that long was in junior high. I thought about what the past year had brought me, where I was in comparison to where I'd been. I was a week out from the one-year anniversary of the infamous bubble bath, the crushing darkness, the heartache, and the overwhelming pain. *How did I get here?*—the question that had played over, and over, in my mind.

I thought about all the moments where I'd felt hopeless, all the moments where I thought, *I'm not going to survive this.*

We don't get to go back in time. We don't get to hop through a portal and reassure the past version of us that it's going to be all right. But I could take a moment to imagine that version of myself—the one who swore she wasn't going to make it through—and reassure her.

Sweet woman, you will survive this. You will survive. You will rebuild. What you're feeling, right now, it is temporary, even though it feels like forever.

I went through my calendar. I set another event notification, exactly one year in the advance. A little note for the future me—the version who'll read that note written by a woman who, by that point, will be an echo, a psychological representation of where she's been.

I wrote out a simple message for the event, the closest thing we've got to a portal through time:

"How are you doing today, you resilient soul? How is life in this chapter? You've come so far. Keep going."

Part X: October

Chapter 40: Interrogate

"Do you ever worry that you're just protecting yourself against romantic love?"

I readjusted in my seat. The interviewer had not been afraid to ask the hard-hitting questions. We were in the final lap of my interview in Raleigh. In the previous hours, we'd talked about my childhood, my relationship hopping, my Year of Dating Myself, and my focus on friendships. In the leadup to her question, the documentarian had noted how I have friends like Britt: gorgeous, smart, engaging women. As a bisexual woman, why *wasn't* I dating her?

Since it had been a question I'd been asked countless times before, I was ready with my answer.

"For me, friendships are friendships. Platonic love is just as sacred. It's not a diluted version of the real thing. That love is special in their own right," I'd said. "I've never had a friendship become a romantic partnership. If I love someone platonically, that's how I love them, period."

That was when the interviewer replied with: "Do you ever worry that you're just protecting yourself against romantic love?"

"With Britt? No. Protecting myself in general?" I paused. "As my therapist reminded me, I'm still healing. In some ways, I'm only

THE YEAR OF DATING MYSELF

just now really getting a chance to build myself up. Maybe I'm protecting myself against romantic love, but that's also what's needed. Right now, I need to heal."

Sunday afternoon slowly shifted into evening as my interview started to wrap up. Britt was already on her flight home to see her children, and Danielle was preparing to drive into town so we could have dinner that evening.

"So, you're currently dating yourself," said the documentarian. "Have you noticed any changes, as a result?"

"Oh, a ton!" I answered. "There were so many things that used to intimidate me, and now I barely think twice about them. I used to cling to people, regardless as to whether or not they were good for me. I felt like I shouldn't have any standards. And now I do."

"You've raised the bar for other people because of what you're doing for yourself," said the documentarian.

"Exactly! Before, it would be like, 'oh, well, it's not like I deserve better, so I won't do anything about it.' Now, I'm willing to draw that line in the sand. I know what I deserve. And, for the first time in my life, I *believe* it too."

"So if you were ever to date someone other than yourself again, do you think you'd date a man again? Or would your preferred partner be a woman?"

I had to pause. One area in my life I'd been navigating was the fact that, even after embracing my queerness, I still primarily dated men. I saw romance through the heterosexual lens. Was there something to my patterns that could be traced back to the default idea that the princess always had a prince?

"I don't know," I said. "I think, for me, it would have to be more about values. Have they been working on themselves? Do they have an empathetic heart? Will they understand that relationships require mutual investment?"

"What about sexually? Who would you prefer to be with?"

"I don't really have an answer to that either," I said. "I don't really have any interest in that right now, so, in some ways, it's a moot point. But I do know that, hypothetically, what I prefer is more energetic than any specific body type. I want to feel safe in their presence. I want to feel like they're attuned to me. I want them to view what we're doing as an intimate act, not a way to gain pleasure at my expense."

I told the documentarian about being on the asexual spectrum, and how life had knocked me deeper into asexuality. I missed my sensuality, but I also wasn't going to force it. I was rebuilding my sense of safety, and that included safety within my own body and mind.

"So, what's next, then?" asked the interviewer.

"Well, I'll continue dating myself," I said, "There's still a few more months left in the year, and I have a bunch of things lined up. So that's what I'm focusing on."

"And, after that?"

I shrugged.

"I guess it's too soon to answer."

Danielle came by as we finished filming. We bid our farewells to the crew and drove to the restaurant.

"Did the interview go well?" Danielle asked as we sat at our table.

"It did!" I scooched my chair in. "She really had me thinking."

The waitress came by to get our drink order. She instantly held my interest. There was something enchanting about her cadence, her mannerisms, and the way she held herself.

"I don't think I'm going to return to dating," I said after the waitress left. "Even after the Year of Dating Myself is complete."

"Oh?" Danielle responded. "I didn't know you'd decided that."

"I mean, it's still an early thought," I faltered, "but I don't think I'm going to return to *active* dating. No dating apps, none of that.

THE YEAR OF DATING MYSELF

If romantic love happens, so be it. But I don't think I'll go looking for it."

"Do you think you'll ever be in a romantic relationship again?"

"I don't know," I answered. "But I do know this: dating is not unlike trying to hire someone for an important job. Ideally, you find the right candidate. But time goes by and no one is the right match and the company feels the strain of this vacancy. Inevitably, you start compromising on what qualifications are needed or what qualities you're looking for. You keep chipping away, compromising until you find someone—anyone—who'd be good enough. I know I've done that in dating, and I never want to do that again."

"Well, I do hope you're willing to give relationships another chance," Danielle said as the waitress came out with our drinks. She chatted with us as we talked about Raleigh. My focus kept coming back to how our waitress spoke, how she moved. There was something endearing about it. But also, so familiar.

As the waitress left our table, I realized exactly what I was looking at.

I was looking at myself.

She joked in the same manner. She did the same head tilt and shoulder shrug. I'd been watching myself through a different set of eyes.

My heart filled.

I thought of all the times that I had called myself awkward. I constantly berated myself for my "weird" mannerisms and wished I could just be "normal" like everyone else. But there I was, witnessing a version of myself, and finding her mannerisms anything but weird.

I smiled and hoped I would never call myself awkward again.

"This has been a really good weekend," I said.

"I agree. And I'm really glad you've been able to heal from your birthday," Danielle continued. "I know how much that had hurt you."

"It did, but . . ." I paused for a moment. "Maybe what was more important of a corrective experience was being able to just let my hurt out with safe people."

"I'm glad you know you have people in your life that you can do that with." Danielle took a sip from her glass. "Now that you're in a better place, I want to admit something. I knew you were hurting, but it also hurt to hear you talk about the weekend like that. I really did everything I could to help save that weekend."

My heart sank.

"I knew you were in a bad place, so I wanted to wait to tell you this," she continued. "But it was like it didn't matter that I was there for you." She paused then added: "Plus, I spent all that money on plane tickets, on food and drinks . . . it's going to take *months* to pay back that credit card."

My breathing went shallow. That was the exact thing I'd worried about: my lack of gratitude that friends had spent money to come see me.

"I wanted you to have a good birthday," said Danielle. "And I really tried. But it was like my contributions didn't matter. You weren't considering me when you talked about how that weekend went."

I thought about Gabe, and the years he felt unconsidered by me.

"I know I'm sensitive to these things," she continued. "I used to have a lot of people in my life who took what I was doing for them for granted."

"Like people wouldn't take you into consideration because *of course* you're going to pick up the slack," I said, saying to Danielle the very things Gabe had once said about himself.

Danielle pressed her lips together. My vision blurred as I got up from my seat, walked around the table, and wrapped Danielle in a tight hug.

"I won't make the same mistake with you as I did with Gabe," I said.

Little did I know that, in the following year, I would look back on that moment in a completely different light. I never could've predicted that, in the year *after* dating myself, Danielle would show a different side: a calculating, merciless side that forced me to look back on our friendship to see if there'd been signs of that side of her.

At that very moment in the restaurant, I thought I was given a chance to not repeat the same mistakes that I'd made with Gabe. I was holding a friend close because I was heartbroken that she felt unappreciated. But, in retrospect, I saw a woman who saw my pain as an affront to her character. I saw a woman who knew how tender the topic of money was—and decided to weaponize that knowledge. I saw a woman who felt slighted because of the insufficient recognition for the hero work that she'd done.

I'd eventually learn in brutal, severe ways that sometimes, the friends who want to be a hero in your life are a double-edged sword—because the amount of work they put into being the hero, they'll just as easily devote to being the villain.

But all you ever wanted was a friend.

I was watching my flight get delayed for the second time when the man across from me asked if I had a charging cord.

"I forgot mine and my earbuds are about to die," he said.

I rummaged through my backpack and gave him a cord to borrow.

"I appreciate that! Thank you!"

"Of course. You're welcome."

The flight attendant at my gate made another announcement. I perked up at the same time as the man.

"Are you on the Boston flight too?" I asked.

"Ah, no. Philadelphia. But it's also out of gate sixteen," he answered.

I nodded politely and went back to my book.

"So, you're from Boston then?" he asked, his energy having shifted.

I closed my eyes, regretting my initial question. A woman quickly learns the difference between a genuine conversation and getting hit on. The questions lose all genuine empathy. The body language becomes more pointed, to the point of aggression.

I answered his questions in a perfunctory manner. I kept my book open, looking back down after each answer, hoping he'd notice.

But that's the thing with being hit on: the person doing it never notices. Because it's not about us as actual people, but as a trophy to capture.

The Philadelphia flight began boarding. I breathed a small sigh of relief. The man unplugged my cord and gave it back to me.

"Thanks again for this," he said. "That should be enough to last me the flight."

"Happy to help," I replied.

The man stood up, grabbed his bag, and looked down at me.

"Hey, can I get your number?"

I bit my tongue, closed my book, and looked up at him.

"I'm sorry," I replied. "I'm taken."

Chapter 41: Hiking

I'd been home for less than a week before I left for my road trip through Maine.

I was making a lifelong dream come true. I was going to hike Mount Katahdin, Maine's highest mountain, which housed Baxter Peak, the northern terminus for the Appalachian Trail. The mountain was a day's drive from me, so I planned to drive up the day before, stay at a nearby inn, and then hike in the morning.

I was also hoping to stop at a restaurant that had one of the few remaining old-fashioned photo booths. I wanted to use one like old-school lovebirds once did.

With my car packed up, I set off for Millinocket, the last town before Baxter State Park, home to Mount Katahdin. I drove for a few hours before pulling off the highway for the restaurant with the photo booth. I parked my car in a suspiciously empty parking lot. I pulled out my phone to confirm that I was in the right place and felt my heart sink.

The restaurant was closed for the week.

"Well, I guess I'm on an adventure to find a place for lunch then!" I said, attempting to cheer myself up. I looked at my route and saw that it went right past Augusta.

THE YEAR OF DATING MYSELF

"I've never been to Augusta, so, why not see what that city has?"

I drove another half hour and pulled off the highway again, to explore Maine's capital. The downtown area was gorgeous, but nothing spoke to me. Outside of downtown, I found only chain restaurants and fast-food options. I looked at my route again and saw I'd also be passing by Bangor. I'd also never been to Bangor, so why not try there too?

After another hour on the road, I pulled into downtown Bangor and immediately found street parking. I took it as my sign to explore the area on foot. I walked around the block, taking in the rushing river and the mural of a man in a red flannel. I found a restaurant that caught my eye and requested a table for one.

There were a lot of things on my mind as I waited for my lunch to arrive. The first was the ease that I'd finally found in going to restaurants *alone*. I remembered how I was practically starving in Québec City. The only times I ate were at fast-food joints or snacks from my car.

The second thought was on the metaphor for the day I was having. Was I disappointed that my original plan fell through? Sure. But, had the restaurant with the photo booth been open, I would've driven past Augusta and Bangor, with no real reason to stop at either city.

But I got to experience both—and I couldn't deny that the adventure was way more fulfilling than a photo booth.

Sometimes the best adventures come from plans gone awry.

I also kept thinking about the mural I'd passed. While I'd later learn that the man in the flannel was supposed to be Paul Bunyan, he was also a dead ringer for someone I'd briefly dated.

The man had been handsome in that rugged, outdoorsy way—as if a Disney prince had decided to take up life as a lumberjack. He was sweet, considerate, and genuine. He was a talented musician and we got along well. I didn't realize it until long after we'd

238

stopped dating, but I'd blindly believed that, because he checked off all the right boxes, we were supposed to date, and I was inevitably going to fall in love.

But, looking back, my fondness for him never stretched into romance.

I thought about the question the documentarian had asked, about dating friends. It was too late, but I'd finally found my answer: checking off all the right boxes does not mean inevitable romance.

The only difference between the women who remained my friends and the men I dated instead was that society had taught me to see dating men as a compulsory act.

How many men had I dated, purely because I was told to "give the *good man* a chance?" How many connections did I try to mold into sexual attraction, because that's what any "real" connection with a man must inevitably lead to? My amazing female friends were spared if only because society was too busy selling me on the prince for her princess.

It's not every day you get to say, "Thanks, compulsory heterosexuality!"

I was finally appreciating all the different ways you can be attracted to someone. Attraction to their intelligence, their energy, or their aesthetics. Attraction to their accomplishments, or even just the camaraderie and connection.

And none of it had to mean you were romantically or sexually attracted to them.

What adventures come when the original plans go awry.

With sunlight fading fast, I made my way back to my car and drove to an inn. My only plan for the night involved lying in bed and watching a TV show that Britt had recommended. I had to get up early the next day and I was wiped out from the day's adventure. I changed into my PJs, set up my hiking gear, and watched a show on the complicated world of dating—specifically, an episode where the love that frees the main character doesn't come from the charming man she meets one morning, but from the friend who embraces the main character for who she is.

I drove to Baxter State Park in the chilly early morning before the sun came up. A small part of me was resistant. In the face of any challenge—even the ones we sign up for—there's always that voice that tempts us into dropping it. I'd learned that it's not a case of trying to shut that voice up, but letting it drone on in the background as you focus on the road ahead of you.

I started power walking through the trail, eyeing the skies, and praying it wouldn't start raining. I wanted to get to the summit while the weather was still good.

Sometimes the universe makes sure that the timing drives home the point. I was remarking that it might be okay if I charged through that trail too—right as I tripped over my feet and pitched forward. My left knee slammed against one rock as my right shin scraped against another. I let out an audible cry and a string of "oh, god*damn*it"s as I got back up and began walking again.

The universe will do whatever it takes to make you learn your damn lesson—and it's not afraid to strike hard when you're not listening.

I slowly went up the mountain, retiring my hiking poles as the trail turned into steep boulders. I hit the ridgeline and focused on each individual step, heavily fatigued but knowing I still had a ways to go. With how the trail curved, I had no idea I was near the summit until I was practically on top of it. I went around a bend by a ledge and, like magic, the infamous sign marking the main peak of Katahdin came into view.

I sat at the peak, watching as other hikers posed with the sign. Some announced that they were thru hikers—people who'd been on the Appalachian Trail for the better part of a year—and had finally completed their journey. It was hard not to get swept up in the emotions of the thru hikers. I gazed at the vista before me, my eyes welling up. I was surrounded by a profound sense of accomplishment, but also an ending.

Every single hiker on that peak—be they thru hikers or day hikers—was on some kind of journey. We all were turning to the trail for *something*. Standing on that peak was like summiting something bigger than ourselves. The first time I ever saw Franconia Notch, I pulled out my notebook and wrote, *The mountains don't make my problems seem small, but they do make my soul feel large.*

We're all just searching for things that remind us of the magnitude of our souls.

I watched a few more thru hikers celebrate their finale. I watched day hikers hand them a beer, a swig from a flask. I got my own photo with the peak's sign before venturing forward onto the Knife Edge trail—a narrow, rocky traverse across the serrated ridge between one peak and the next. I took my time, pausing to take in the sheer drops on either side of me. I was willing to scope out the trail and be deliberate with where I put my feet.

Proof I could learn my damn lesson.

After one final push of outright rock climbing, I hit the mountain range's second peak and prepared for the descent—a descent that I'd chosen because it looked gentle on the map. However, it was anything but gentle. My left knee pulsated as I hobbled down the trail. I watched my pace slow to the point that hikers that I'd passed in the beginning were now passing me by. I went from an hour ahead of schedule to an hour behind.

THE YEAR OF DATING MYSELF

But I let myself take it easy. I tediously got back to the trailhead and breathed a sigh of relief when I sat in my driver's seat and took off my hiking boots. After crudely cleaning myself and changing into a new set of clothes, I began my drive out of the park and back home.

My plan was to drive through the evening, getting home in time for bed. I got to the main gate of the park when I spotted two of the thru hikers that I'd seen on the peak. One of them caught my eye and walked over to my car.

"Hey, the hostel that was supposed to pick us up left us stranded instead. Is there any way you'd be able to give us a ride?"

I immediately started moving my stuff from my passenger seat.

"Of course!" I said, so focused on clearing a space for two hikers that I forgot that I was still on the main road and holding up traffic. The ranger had to tap on my window and ask me to pull to the side.

"Thank you so much for this," said the first hiker as we started driving back to town.

"Really, I'm happy to help," I answered.

As we made our way down the road, the hikers—friends who'd met on the trail—talked about their journey.

"So, what's next for you, now that you're done?" the second hiker—who'd introduced herself by her trail name Sunshine—asked the first hiker.

"I'm moving to California," said the first, who went by the trail name Hummingbird. "With absolutely no plan!"

"Well, after doing what you just did, that'll be nothing by comparison," said Sunshine.

"That's my thinking," Hummingbird replied. "Like, I just slept on the side of a highway. I've proven I can survive anything."

I held onto that dialogue long after I dropped off Sunshine and Hummingbird at the hostel and drove through the night. When we prove that we can survive the toughest challenges—whether by choice or by fate—everything else shifts in perspective. When we've been to hell and back, the problems in the mortal world seem so much tamer. What are we looking for on the trail, on solo journeys, on quests to expand when our circumstances demand we shrink?

We're looking for proof that the world around us is nothing compared to our inner strength.

I returned home with a throbbing knee. I hobbled up the stairs and into bed, too exhausted to even take a shower. I had left it all on the trail—and, in emptying myself out, I'd made room for something better.

Chapter 42: Shine

"Did I ever dull your shine?"

I almost didn't know what to do with the question Gabe had asked.

"What do you mean?"

Gabe shared something his girlfriend had said: previously, she'd been with men who "dulled her shine," who told her to tone it down when she got excited about things.

"Did I ever do that to you?" he asked. "To clarify, not the times I told you that it had nothing to do with you, and that I was over-stimulated. Times I just told you to tone it down."

I could see how he drew parallels between his girlfriend and me. We had similar personalities. The number of times I'd watch them interact and remark to Gabe with a knowing smile, "you have a type."

(It wasn't me staking my claim. That had been his type before I came into the picture, and it continued to be his type even after.)

"I mean, yes and no," I replied. "When you found the wording to explain you were just overstimulated, it stopped. But before that, it was more like, 'you need to tone it down.'"

THE YEAR OF DATING MYSELF

"I'm sorry for that then," he replied. "It was never my intention."

"I know," I said. "I don't blame you for it. We were kids. We didn't have the knowhow. Once we knew better, we did better."

"You know what our problem was?" Gabe said after a moment. "Our problem was getting married."

I shrugged.

"Getting married meant a lot to you," I replied.

"Yeah, but you told me that you never wanted to get married."

"But that was back when I didn't think I had any autonomy," I countered. "It wasn't, 'I don't want to get married, and therefore I won't.' It was just, 'I don't want to get married.'"

"Which meant you thought you'd be getting married, regardless."

"Yup," I said. "I knew you wanted to get married, I was supposed to get married anyway . . . it made sense, back then."

Where would we be, if we'd never gotten married? Maybe we would've continued on, decades upon decades as boyfriend and girlfriend, like Goldie Hawn and Kurt Russel. But I knew that was too simplistic. It was like when I'd tell people that we'd broken up because Gabe wanted to have children and I didn't.

Fairytales teach us how beautiful it is to sacrifice for love. But something gets lost in translation between the knight sacrificing his life and the layperson sacrificing what they want out of life. The reasons we broke up were layered and complicated, but a major factor was that we had both molded ourselves to be what the other wanted. We both lost our identities trying to make our disjointed puzzle pieces fit. We spent years fighting the inevitable truth: the marriage was only functional when we played our respective roles.

And we'd outgrown those roles long ago.

Major personal sacrifice in the name of love creates a "Gift of the Magi": hacking off or giving away parts of ourselves to better our partner's life, while ultimately rendering ourselves without the tools needed to accept what they give to us.

We were once kids who attended each other's college graduations before meeting each other at the altar. We fumbled forward, meaning no harm but ultimately harming the other. We eventually grew into the best versions of ourselves, but it was a Pyrrhic victory. The past was too big, with too much pain and too much baggage tied to it.

But I also knew that had we met in the present day, I would most likely regard him in the exact same way as I do now: my intellectual match and one of the best people I knew. But not someone I wanted to date.

I thought about our wedding vows, the traditional Christian promise to love, to honor, and to cherish. While the rings we gave each other sat in boxes gathering dust, our vows, in some ways, were still being honored. He was still someone I loved, honored, and cherished. Someone I'd always be around for, in sickness and in health, for richer or for poorer. Maybe not as the lawfully wedded wife, but as a best friend.

I know that friendship is not what society expects after the end of a marriage. I know, for some, my situation will always be "worthy" of a side-eye. But I also know that, when I stopped trying to cram our bond into an ill-fitting romantic box, I was more able to fully feel that love.

Ideally, a love that I will have for the rest of my life, 'til death do us part.

I heard the song again on the radio.

The Christian song, the one that brought me back to my patient zero, the heartbreak that kickstarted my frenzied dating life. I heard

THE YEAR OF DATING MYSELF

it as I drove back from a solo coffee date. I listened to the song and let its impact be felt.

Neither of us were looking for a relationship, patient zero and I. We'd been effectively paired up on a blind date by a well-meaning friend who thought we'd be great together. We were nonchalant about the date. He even ended up running late because the hike he was on took longer than expected.

"Which hike did you do today?" I asked when we finally met up.

His answer was my favorite mountain trail.

We peppered the date with knowing looks at the other, silently and simultaneously acknowledging the chemistry between us. We ended the date with a noncommittal agreement to hang out again and a hug that lasted longer than it should've.

A week later we ran into each other at a hiking trailhead.

Neither of us were looking for anything, which might've been why everything was able to flourish. There was no pressure to force the connection into any unnatural shape, and so it expanded. We talked about that expansion, about what that connection meant. We were both on board for what the future might hold. But then reality set in for him, and I refused to accept our new reality.

After everything was said and done, I tried for a friendship with him. But the same patterns emerged. He was open and proactive, so long as I was aloof and guarded. But all it took was the hint of my walls coming back down and he'd disappear again. We were a year past our breakup when he finally admitted that he was in love with me and didn't know how to handle it.

He was the dog chasing the car, devoted to the cause so long as there was no hope of catching up with the vehicle. But heaven knows what he'd do if the car stopped.

I eventually blocked his number. The last I'd heard from him was via a text message that had been blocked on my phone, but somehow made it to the messenger app on my laptop:

"Hey! How's things? Haven't seen much of you online these days so I wanted to see how you're doing. I miss you!"

I never replied.

As I pulled into my driveway that cold October morning, where the Christian song had transported me back in time—as I replayed what that relationship had been for me—I felt a tenderness in my heart. I'd proclaimed to love several men after patient zero. None of those proclamations proved to be true. I'd felt many things—infatuation, limerence, a trauma bond—but, once the dust settled, it was clear that I hadn't fallen *in love* with any of them.

But I had truly fallen in love with my patient zero.

I felt a warmth swirl in my chest. In a way, I still loved him. I would probably always love him.

Where others would feel despair in such a realization, I felt hope.

Romantic love still existed in me, even if it was only an echo.

I closed my garage door and got out of my car. I had no idea what he was up to these days, but I hoped he was doing well. I hoped his dating life had been kind to him, and I hoped that he'd found the healing needed to stop running from love that feels too big.

Chapter 43: Undertake

"Only fifty-six years it took, to find the right man!" the photographer sheepishly remarked as her partner helped with setting up.

I'd been hired as her model for a jewelry company. It was the sixth or seventh time I'd done a photoshoot with her, but it was the first time she had help. Her boyfriend diligently organized the jewelry, adjusted the lighting, and took cues from the photographer with a loyal smile.

The photographer's statement stayed with me, long after the photoshoot wrapped. My mind was split, processing the statement from two opposite ends of the spectrum. On the one hand, love can happen at any time, and there's never a point where it's too late for true, compatible, respectful love. On the other hand, trustworthy love is such a rare gem—surrounded by so many fakes and frauds and costume jewelry that turns your skin green—that it can take over fifty years to find even one.

After the photo shoot, I drove to the city's downtown area. I wandered the main street until a restaurant caught my eye and I requested a table for one. As it became a ritual for me, I immediately compared the moment to Québec City, and how far I'd come since my first solo trip. I had gotten braver. I had become more confident. Friends noticed light returning to my eyes.

"You're not just doing a year of dating yourself," Britt told me. "You're doing a year of living life. You want to do an adventure and you just do it."

A few weeks after Katahdin, Britt took herself out to dinner and was overwhelmed with the confidence boost it gave her—to have the booth to herself, to claim space with her knee up and her foot on the bench. It's hard to fully explain what shifts when you decide you can take yourself to the things you want to do—that you can treat yourself the way you always wanted to be treated. Something in your core solidifies. You stand with yourself as you take yourself out.

I compared recent photos to those from the year before. Yes, the light was back in my eyes, but there was something *more*. There was a sharpness to them—the kind of sharpness that dares you to doubt what she can do.

I pulled up to the fencing academy, ready to turn around.

Despite my fervent search for a class—and my relief at finding one that was only one hour away instead of two—it was just far enough outside of my comfort zone that it made me want to run. My vow to Lana that I'd do the class in Samuel's honor was the main thing that kept me moving forward out of my car, into the building, and toward my class. The instructor was kind and smiled brightly when I told him that it was my very first class. I followed him to the gear closet where I put on the chest protector and was fitted for a helmet.

As we started warm-ups, I became acutely aware of just how outside of that comfort zone I truly was. I had a background in kickboxing, but the rules were reversed for fencing. The stance was the opposite. The large, sweeping motions needed for a punch left me vulnerable to attack. But I watched how patient and understanding everyone was. Before long, I could barely suppress my smile as I shuffled and lunged alongside my partner.

"I hope you had fun!" the instructor said as the class wound down.

"I did!" I replied.

I took off my gear as some of the students lingered to spar. There was a huge, unwavering smile on my face as I said my goodbyes and went to my car and told Lana all about it.

"Samuel would've been so happy that he inspired one of your adventures," said Lana.

"His memory continues to be a blessing," I said, as I felt the tears well up.

I drove home thinking about how the class unlocked something in me. There was a fencing academy that was only a twenty-minute drive from me, one that offered beginner classes, so long as I was willing to sign up for an eight-week series. I'd dismissed the idea, if only because I didn't want to be locked into seven additional classes if the first one didn't work out. But, after that fencing class, I was curious as to when their next series started.

We step outside of our comfort zones for exactly these moments—when we find out that our restrictions are not set in stone, and we can jostle them free. We become the goldfish that has been given a bigger tank and permission to grow a little more. Our doubts blur into the background and our abilities come a little more into focus, helping us see what else is within our wheelhouse.

Life is short. Life is *despairingly* short. And unpredictable. And tough. We have no choice but to jostle those restrictions. Our spirit can only grow according to the size of the container it's in.

THE YEAR OF DATING MYSELF

I had a late-night class on Halloween, but I celebrated the holiday the weekend before. I adorned my home with the fall decorations that I hadn't used in years. I found a near-perfect pumpkin and tried my hand at carving a more ornate jack-o'-lantern. I hadn't made a jack-o'-lantern in years and had never ventured outside of the traditional triangle shapes cut with a kitchen knife.

As I used tools meant for pumpkin carving, I was amazed at how much fun it was to get lost in the design. In the past, there'd always been an anxious franticness about pumpkin carving, like I couldn't finish it fast enough, like I couldn't wait to abandon my jack-o'-lantern with their toothy smile and reminder that I wasn't "good" at pumpkin carving.

Amazing, what happens, when we're strong enough to slow it down and stay present in our experience.

But, still, I couldn't help but look forward. November was around the corner. I had two months left in the Year of Dating Myself. I had a few things lined up for November, but December was sparse.

In particular, I had no New Year's Eve plans.

As far as I knew, Georgia wasn't planning another New Year's trip—and, even if she were, it wasn't a smart idea to assume I could impose on it. Plus, waiting for others to make plans was counterintuitive to what the entire year was about. I thought about what would make a fitting bookend for the year, and I arrived at exactly one conclusion.

It was the place I kept referencing back to: my first solo trip, my ill-fated weekend in Québec City, just before leaving my last relationship.

I'd originally envisioned the trip as my chance to finally see the beautiful city and prove how independent I was. Instead, I cried on my drive there. I frantically walked around. I spent my nights in my room. I fought back tears on the drive home, waiting at the border crossing like I was in line for execution. I checked my phone when I was back in the US, only to see my then-boyfriend on a livestream with another woman, flirting, laughing, and acting like the Prince Charming I once had, with an affable energy that I hadn't received in months.

I spent my drive through the White Mountains screaming into my steering wheel, convinced I was going crazy.

Maybe I wasn't as desperate for corrective experiences as I'd been before, but Québec City still needed a redo. There were restaurants I'd walked past that deserved a visit. There was a scenic drive that deserved my full attention. I'd heard that Québec City was beautiful in the winter—that its snowy majesty is worth the frigid temperatures. I searched online and booked a new room, using my previous experience of the neighborhoods to make a more informed choice than the first time I visited.

I kept saying, "Québec City deserves another chance," before stopping myself.

It wasn't that the city deserved another chance, but that *I* deserved to return as a new and improved version of myself. Like visiting your high school when you're in college, excited to show your favorite teacher how much you've grown; how your life's been since you sat at one of their desks. I was returning to the first place where I'd attempted to steer my own ship. It was only right to show that place the proficiency I'd gained since then.

As I confirmed my booking, I felt something settle in my soul.

I was going to be in Québec City for New Year's. I was going to finish the year in the place where it all started, months before I knew what kind of journey I would officially undertake.

Part XI: November

Chapter 44: Magic

I canceled the first date I'd planned for November.

Back in the spring, I'd purchased a ticket for a string quartet performance, lit by candlelight. But I'd bought the ticket before I'd registered for my fall semester and before I started weekly physical therapy at the physical therapy clinic on campus.

And I had both during the time slot slated for the performance.

I didn't want to cancel my date, but I knew it was the right choice. We were finally making some progress in PT, and my only option would've been to cancel. Attendance was mandatory in my graduate program, and it was a course in which every class mattered. There was a reason *Maintain your 4.0* was on my Solo Tour list. Prioritizing education was just as important as anything else, and I'd already faltered in keeping a proper focus on my coursework.

There'll be other performances, I told myself. I imagined how I'd respond if my partner had class on an evening that I'd planned something. I'd be saying exactly that, honoring just how important their education was to them. I tried to hold back a parallel memory, but holding back a thought is like holding back the water in a garden hose: all you're doing is building up pressure.

I remembered how my ex asserted that, once he was famous, I could just stay home and write all day—and how my heart sank at his words. I was halfway through my master's at that point, and deeply passionate about my field. Anyone who knew me would've known I had no interest in abandoning it. It was clear, even then, how much he didn't *see* me.

I was frustrated. *Why* was I orbiting that old memory? I was tired of moving in circles.

I begrudgingly reminded myself that moving forward doesn't mean that the past stops affecting you. I can move forward and tend to lingering injuries simultaneously.

I was allowed to process—and a need to process didn't negate my progress.

I went to PT. I attended class. I was grateful for both. I went home afterward and curled up in bed.

Sometime in October, Stella had alerted me that my ex was posting photos with his arms unsettlingly around a nineteen-year-old singer in a show he was a part of. I knew it was inevitable. I was doing my best to remember that you can't stop them all, and you can't save every victim. Karma might be the last to bat, but you don't get to choose when—or how—it comes to the plate. I had to make peace with that.

I'd never heard from the young woman again, even after her promise to call. I could only hope she'd found some healing in everything.

"I don't think I want any more updates," I eventually told Stella, after sitting with the exhaustion, the disappointment, and the weight of a world where there's little comeuppance for charismatic men.

For me, it was proof that I could move forward and hold space for pain at the same time.

I saw the email and my heart dropped.

The tattoo artist had finally sent me her design of the Greek goddess Artemis. I'd given her a thorough description, with meticulously labeled reference photos. I'd left no stone unturned in explaining it. But in that email, instead of a version of that vision, I'd gotten a trace of one of the reference photos, shoehorned into place and looking nothing like what I'd described.

I went over my original email multiple times, wondering if I'd miscommunicated.

I was disappointed. I was frustrated. I'd been wanting the tattoo of Artemis—my favorite goddess, my patron goddess, the namesake of one of my cats—for years. I'd methodically researched tattoo artists, painstakingly picking someone I thought would do the Greek deity justice. And yet, just days away from my long-awaited appointment, disappointment was what I got.

But it was so much more than that. I was, yet again, in a situation where the ball had been dropped and I would have to stand up for myself.

And I was *tired* of it.

What part of wanting softness was the universe not understanding?

There was more to this frustration, something I didn't notice until I talked with Britt about it. I'd drained myself, explaining to the artist what I wanted. I'd taken great care to provide so much information that the artist wouldn't have had to do any research. I spelled everything out so that the only thing the artist would have to do is *pay attention*.

What I got, in return, was a sign that I wasn't even heard.

That had been my dating life, in a nutshell. The ways I destroyed myself, spelling everything out for the men I was with. All they had to do was pay attention, but I couldn't even get that. Their actions were like a lazy trace of someone else's work.

I told the artist my thoughts and explained to her that what she'd shown me had missed the mark. The artist apologized, and I was quick to become self-deprecating.

"That was probably my fault," I wrote in my reply. "I did myself a disservice, sending such a lengthy explanation, the way that I did."

It made me wonder if the parallel to my dating life extended there, as well. Had my overinvestment set the stage for minimal input? Did working myself to the bones enable a sense of laziness? Were my volumes of effort a signal that they didn't need to even hold up a page?

I didn't have an answer. All I knew was, if it was not immediately corrected, I was willing to walk away from my tattoo appointment.

Which, at least, was where the situation differed from my dating life.

I anxiously waited for the artist's revisions. I was firm in my resolve; I was willing to cancel my appointment and lose my deposit. Better a financial loss than to gain something that I didn't love. But the artist pulled through, presenting me almost exactly what I was looking for, if not better. I knew it was my reward—be it from a higher power or just the natural laws of cause and effect—for sticking up for myself.

But I was *tired* of demonstrating lessons learned. I was *tired* of lessons, in general.

I was *tired* of growth.

I was so *tired*. I didn't want to do it anymore.

I walked into the tattoo parlor on a blustering November morning. I picked at my cuticles, taking deliberate breaths as the needle met my skin.

I thought about the goddess Artemis and her mythology. Goddess of the hunt, one who shows up arrogant men and saves women from sexual assault. She was the maiden goddess. Even when in love with Orion, she refused to share her body with him.

Artemis was more than my favorite character in folklore. She was a symbol of protection. She stood for something that I aspired toward. But I had to wonder if my path was starting to look a little too identical to hers.

Was I fated to be the maiden mortal? Ready to show down, ready to protect, but with her body locked away?

I had no answers for that.

Before I knew it, the artist finished.

I stood in the mirror with a satisfied smile. It was worth all the work of asserting what I wanted for the design, even if I wished I'd never had to do it in the first place. The Greek goddess drew back her bow and arrow in the light of a crescent moon. Her stag antlers grazed against my shoulder blade. Delicate vines pulled everything together.

I finally had my own symbol of the protector. The maiden goddess.

I still had a few hours left on my metered parking, but I decided against taking myself for a celebratory dinner with the remaining time. I was already starting to shiver, a sign that my adrenaline—spiked from getting the tattoo—was crashing. I decided what I needed more than a toast to myself was something warm, cozy, and familiar before the inevitable bottoming out.

"I got a new tattoo, then two days later I went to a rock concert. Suffice it to say, I'm living my best life," I told Britt.

Just a few days after my tattoo appointment, I drove down to Boston, returning to a music venue that I once frequented, back when I was getting my bachelor's degree. I told Lindsey that I was too old for a standing room only concert. But there is something

THE YEAR OF DATING MYSELF

undeniable about general admission concerts. It amplifies the feeling of the collective. Within the first few chords of the music, individual people become a unified whole, singing and cheering in unison. Whether or not you came with someone becomes insignificant. You become a molecule in a more complex organism.

I left the venue after the concert—my ears ringing and my skin vibrating with joy—and decided to walk the mile to my old college campus. I was so ecstatic that I started skipping down the sidewalk. I thought about my orientation leader, freshman year, warning us to never walk that area at night. It was an outdated warning, even back then. Even at midnight, the sidewalks were filled with college students and baseball fans.

I started passing university-owned buildings, slowly entering the main campus. I walked past the university's convenience store and couldn't help but stare. Once upon a time, an eighteen-year-old me thought it was so novel that she could use her dining hall pass like a credit card there.

I crossed the street, and my heart suddenly became heavy. Once upon a time, I was "eighteen-year-old me." I was fresh out of high school and had just spent the summer in correspondence with a future classmate. I fell in puppy love with him when we met in person. I clung to him with both hands while he had one eye on his high school ex-girlfriend and the other on a fraternity. When I was finally too heartbroken to continue our vaguely defined relationship, I dove into dating, eager to replace him.

I had to smirk. My patterns stretched further back than I'd thought.

The fevered college dating had left me with only heartache and disappointment. I cried in my dorm room after getting stood up on Valentine's Day. I told myself that enough was enough—that I was letting romance clog my mind. I had a scholarship to maintain. It was time to swear off dating until after I graduated.

Four days later, I met Gabe.

I held that parallel gently as I returned to my car. Back then, breaking my vow against dating had resulted in one of the best people entering my life.

Could I really blame myself, then, for hoping history would repeat itself?

I'd scrambled to replace patient zero. I'd sworn off dating, only to cling to the first man who'd potentially fit the bill. When that didn't work out, I repeated the pattern again. And again. And again.

Insanity is doing the same thing, over and over again, expecting a different outcome, but perhaps I'd been hoping to recapture the magic from my freshman year. But magic isn't something to be captured, let alone recaptured. You could try to return to that world, but—just like visiting your alma mater, years after you've graduated—you're only a guest in that space.

I drove home, remembering the last time I ever spoke to the boy I had puppy love for: we'd just graduated, and he'd just caught wind that I was engaged. He'd sent a message, congratulating me. He attempted to take credit for me meeting my fiancé, his logic painfully flimsy. There was a jitteriness to his words. I couldn't shake the feeling that he was trying to evade his regret of letting me slip through his fingers.

That had once mattered to me. After he'd broken my heart, I'd wanted him to regret his actions. But, by the time he did, I had no use for it.

"The one that got away" is just a reminder that some people are capable of appreciating magic only after the show is over.

Chapter 45: Tour's End

About a week before Thanksgiving—and a week before Britt was to come visit—I updated my Solo Tour jacket.

The blank sleeves of the denim jacket that Stella made became filled with dates. Stella had designed a similar jacket for Britt. Three friends, all single, all deciding to focus on themselves. It was something to be proud of. A sporadic idea on New Year's Eve had evolved into something beyond what I could've expected. *I* had evolved beyond what I could've expected. A lot had caught up with me, but I'd learned none of it had been unbeatable.

But I started to receive one *specific* question: "What are you going to do once the year is over?"

"Keep dating myself!" was my canned response—which was true. I wanted to keep taking myself on adventures, keep trying new things, and keep investing in myself.

"But do you think you'll stay *single?*"

I had no solid answer. The only thing I knew was that I wasn't returning to dating apps.

I'd joined an online group, a sisterhood of women to vet potential dates. So many of the posts were grim: women gave dire warnings about the cheaters, the abusers, and the people who were secretly

THE YEAR OF DATING MYSELF

married. The group was doing what it was designed to do: protect women. But it also reminded me of how dangerous the dating world can be. My ache for affectionate touch and romantic love was still present, but it also felt like a siren's call.

And I wasn't about to dash myself on the rocks.

On a crisp afternoon, as I walked out of the art museum that I'd taken myself to, I overheard an argument. I kept my eyes diverted as I walked across the parking lot, pretending I didn't hear the woman and man. I tried my best not to project my experiences onto them, but I couldn't help but hear the exasperated pleading in her voice and the belligerence in his. Out of the corner of my eye, I watched him throw his hands up and walk away, as she followed right behind him.

I got in my car and sighed. Yes, I ached for romantic love, but it felt like aching for a unicorn. I never wanted to plead for a partner to listen to me, ever again. I never wanted to pour myself out to someone who'd just throw their hands up and turn their back when they weren't getting their way.

Perhaps that is why fairy tales were made in the first place.

We desire something that rarely plays out in reality. So, the poets write about beautiful orchids in the snow—all the while knowing that, in the real world, the orchid would be quick to wither and die in such conditions.

Chapter 46: Freedom

"My ex-husband has the kids for Thanksgiving, I really don't want to be around my family for Thanksgiving . . . why don't I come out to see you?"

I originally planned to fly out to see Britt for her birthday, which was right before Thanksgiving. But instead, she flew in to celebrate her birthday and Thanksgiving with me.

For Britt's birthday, I brought us to the paint bar that was right next to the theater. I'd been meaning to go to that paint bar as a solo date, but never got around to it. Britt had a deep love for painting, and it was in confirming her birthday plans that I was grateful that I'd pushed off the date. It was something I wanted to experience for the first time with Britt by my side.

Sometimes you realize there was a reason for the delay. Sometimes what feels like being held back is actually a way to synchronize the timing.

On the way to the paint bar, Britt and I discussed her dating life. We talked about the woman that she'd been pursuing, only to realize that the effort was one-sided.

THE YEAR OF DATING MYSELF

"Honestly, when I stop letting my loneliness control me, I'm disgusted at the idea of romance," Britt admitted. "I don't want that anxiety in my life again."

I thought about that feeling—that pang of jealousy, insecurity, and fear. The way your heart clenches when you realize they don't feel the same.

I missed the euphoria, the giddiness. I missed seeing another mortal as something divine. But I didn't miss that other side of the coin. I didn't miss the anxiety, the worry. I didn't miss the way your spirit deflates when your beloved has eyes for someone else.

We were only one of two tables for the paint bar that night— perhaps a casualty of the holidays. The other table hosted a couple out on a date. Upon hearing the girlfriend's conversation with the instructor as she gathered their paint supplies, it was clear that she had organized the date. I watched the guy's low energy and enthusiasm and tried my best not to assume the worst: that the girlfriend had jumped through hoops for a bonding experience with a man who couldn't be bothered.

Britt and I watched our paintings come to life. We both lamented how terrible we were at blending the colors—how our nervous hands and overthinking minds always resulted in clear, delineated blocks of color.

Life is poetry, even when you're not sure what the metaphor means.

I showed Britt around my college campus the next day— something I had wanted to do over my birthday, but had been canceled alongside brunch—and talked about my master's degree. I was a semester away from starting my fieldwork. Slowly, my master's was manifesting in my hands.

We spent Thanksgiving in easy laziness. It was a new and disorienting experience for Britt, but, for me, it was old hat. I hadn't celebrated Thanksgiving the "traditional" way in years.

Before my father passed, I would brace myself and spend the day with my family. The year my father died, I attempted to host a Thanksgiving dinner for my mom and brother. I ended up in tears by the sink afterward, washing dishes with Gabe and swearing I'd never host another Thanksgiving again.

And I never did. I also never attended another traditional Thanksgiving. From then on out, Gabe and I opted to stay home, order takeout, and watch movies. Even with the dissolution of our marriage, the ritual remained.

In the afternoon, Gabe came by with a large bag of Chinese takeout. After we had our fill, we piled into Gabe's truck and drove north.

Nina—the woman who'd been my first girlfriend before becoming one of my closest friends—was spending Thanksgiving with her sons and her coparenting partner. She'd invited us to play board games and we'd happily accepted.

It was an unorthodox Thanksgiving. There I was with Britt and the man I was once married to, visiting the woman I once dated, to play board games with her own unique family arrangement.

I had no use for the social script, the one that declared that interpersonal dynamics had to exist in specific molds. As I sat on the couch with my eclectic chosen family—as I watched Nina and Gabe catch up with each other, and Nina and Britt bond instantly, and as I rested my head against Nina's during the pauses in the video game we played with her sons—I thought about how faint the ache for romantic love was in that moment.

Did I really yearn to be in romantic love again, or was I reaching for it in times when my well of connection was running dry? How badly would I ache for the embrace of a lover if my platonic beloveds were all within proximity to me?

A nutritionist friend had once talked about craving certain junk foods because of a vitamin deficiency. Was I craving a fairy-tale love when my internal system was only trying to address a deficiency in connection?

I was reminded why I was only dating myself. I once thought questions like, "How will I ever trust again after abuse?" would knock the wind out of me. In reality, that honor belonged to questions like:

"Do I miss romance because I miss it, or because I was *taught* that it was the only way to feel truly connected to someone?"

My younger brother called me that night.

"Happy Thanksgiving!" said my brother.

"Happy Thanksgiving to you too! How've things been at home?"

As I paced around my house, my brother told me about getting on an Alzheimer's facility waitlist. Our mother was getting worse. She'd had a few falls. She'd let out my brother's dog, having forgotten that there wasn't a gate to keep him in the yard. The dog was eventually found, but not after getting into a fight with another dog and biting its owner. The owner refused to press charges, but they lived in a state where multiple dog bites resulted in mandatory euthanasia.

"I don't know if I'll admit her once I get to the top of the list," said my brother. "I'm allowed to let others skip ahead of me, which I think I'll do. But . . . it's bad. I don't want to be in a place where I have to wait if something really big happens."

It was a long time coming. My brother had been doing whatever he could to keep her out of a nursing home. Others would've given up sooner.

I know I would've.

The most heartbreaking element of Alzheimer's is its inevitability. There's no comeback story, no tale of redemption. There's no salvation in the eleventh hour.

There's just deterioration.

You cannot hope for miracles. You can only hope for mercy.

I responded calmly, as if he'd just told me about his Thanksgiving dinner. Perhaps most people would've seen it as me taking the news in stride—that "level head" that my first therapist would always remark on.

But the look on Britt's face showed me how disconnected I was.

"I would like to give you a hug right now," she said, and held me close. The tears instantly slid down my face.

I'd meant to visit my brother and my mom in September. The events of the summer had rendered me too exhausted to even consider it. I'd never been one to blindly champion seeing family. What misguided advice, depending on who you talk to.

My father was proof that "they'll be gone someday" is sometimes reassurance, not a threat.

But I knew I needed to visit. I could feel it. My mom wouldn't remember it. But a stirring in my soul told me I needed it. I'd finally become the version of me that my upbringing had deprived me of. I needed that version of me to give my hometown a proper sendoff.

I drove Britt to the airport a few days later.

"Remember when we were worried that this would be too much time together, and now we're wanting just one more day?" I asked, trying to make light of our heavy emotions.

We made tentative plans to see each other in the new year. We joined the throngs of other people wishing their family off after Thanksgiving, the pang of knowing your community isn't physically in your community. I came home and felt the sharpness of an empty house. What are our hearts but boats set adrift, desperate for land again?

I pulled out my phone and texted my brother.

"Hey, when is a good time for me to visit?"

Part XII: December

Chapter 47: Vacancy

I put up Christmas decorations before my next solo date.

I hadn't decorated for Christmas in years. My father had been rushed to the ER right after Thanksgiving in what would turn out to be his last year. On his second day in the hospital, he had a grand mal seizure, his alcohol withdrawal so severe that he was transferred to the intensive care unit.

I clung to Christmas that year, as if the boughs of holly would pull me out of the anguish and despair. The following Christmas—with my father gone, my marriage on the rocks, and life rendering me into a crisis—I tried again with holiday cheer. I strung up lights to fight the darkness. I breathed in the tree and prayed the pine smell would take me away.

It's hard to say if the attempt succeeded or failed. What did happen was that I equated Christmas cheer with crushing, suffocating darkness—a darkness I would experience again in a bubble bath after leaving my last relationship—and I gave up trying.

I still wasn't in the Christmas spirit, but I decided that the Year of Dating Myself was going to be a year that I brushed the dust off the boughs of holly. With my decorating complete, I made the long,

THE YEAR OF DATING MYSELF

backroads drive to the cottage I'd been wanting to visit for months—the home that had been renovated into a fixed-price luncheon spot.

Earlier in the week, when I'd called to make my reservation and they'd asked how many people, I'd heard myself squeak out an apologetic, "Oh, only one!"

All my progress, and I was *still* treating going alone as if it were bad news. It was something I needed to nip. Dating myself was not the consolation prize after striking out with romance. That kind of mindset, no matter how subtle, was going to set me up if I ever decided to be with someone again.

If the peace of my own presence was treated as second tier, I ran a high risk of destroying my peace for whatever I think is on the first.

I walked into the cottage, shaking off the cold. The hostess checked my reservation and verified that it was "just *one*."

"Yup, just one!" I said, mirroring her words, but trying to give some confidence to them.

I sat at my table and the waitress came up.

"Are you waiting for anyone else?" she asked.

"Oh no, it's just me today," I said, wondering why I couldn't ax the word "just" from my vocabulary.

"That's totally okay!" said the waitress, clearing the other placemat. "I'm sorry I assumed otherwise!"

"No worries. I imagine there aren't many tables for one."

"Oh, you'd be surprised!" the waitress replied. "A lot of single people come in and dine alone."

Something about the phrase "single people" made me twitch.

"Personally, I love that," the waitress continued. "I was just telling my daughter—she's back for winter break—I told her, 'Go into town! You can do things without your friends!' Trying to foster some independence in her, y'know?"

"It's an important thing to have," I said, "to be able to enjoy your own company."

"Yup! And boy do I enjoy my own company too," she said, before taking my drink order.

Much like on the dinner train, the five-course meal came out in measured beats. I savored each portion. Being in the final weeks of my fall semester, I'd been subsisting on snacks. It was the first proper meal I'd had in a while.

Afterward, I wandered the grounds. I entered the gift shop and picked up a few Christmas gifts. *Have big dreams and grow into them*, read one pendant. A wooden sign hung next to the cash register read, *The greatest adventure is what lies ahead.*

I meandered outside. It was cold and overcast, but something was reminding me of the Christmas spirit. Perhaps it was the holiday music gently coming through the speakers. Perhaps it was the lights and the Christmas-themed gifts. Or perhaps it was the understanding that there was a reason so many cultures celebrated that time of year with lights and music and reminders of joy.

In the darkest of times, you have to create your own light.

I was ready to drive home when I realized I was a town over from a chocolate shop that had once meant the world to me. I pulled up the shop's address and set off.

It had been years since I last visited the shop. It had once been a frequent stop with Gabe. The place meant so much to us that we hired them to make our wedding favors when we got married. The shop represented something young, naïve, and whimsical.

I *had* to return.

I thought about the building—the gorgeous redbrick that also housed a bookstore, down the hall from the shop. It was all I could think about when I pulled into a strip mall parking lot, my GPS concluding that I'd reached my destination.

THE YEAR OF DATING MYSELF

"No, that can't be right," I said.

I looked over and saw the chocolate shop's name, clear as day. I searched online and found that my GPS had not steered me wrong.

It was *the* chocolate shop.

They'd moved.

I could feel the weight of looming symbolism as I walked in. I enjoyed candy in small doses, but Gabe loved chocolate. I walked over to the display case and ordered a box for him. He was out of town for work but was due back within the week. The chocolates would hold until then. The young woman on the other side of the counter rang up my order. I was tempted to ask when they'd moved, but chickened out. She was so young, and it had been so long since I'd last been there. There was a chance it was the only location she knew.

I walked back to my car, placed the chocolates on my passenger seat, and sighed. Times change, and things change with it. I drew the parallels between an old era of my life and a beloved candy store in a bewilderingly new location.

How expensive the rent must've been in the redbrick building. The economy was a much different landscape than it was fifteen years ago. I imagined the owners made the decision to move, lest they go out of business.

Not unlike how Gabe and I ended our marriage, lest the friendship die with it.

Sometimes change is morally neutral. Neither good nor bad, but an adaptation.

Sometimes the world shifts and you just can't go back.

It was getting late. The sun had long set. But I remembered where the downtown area was and decided to return to the redbrick building—return to a place that once held that whimsy. I felt a similar bewilderment when I pulled into a parking spot near the

280

redbrick building. Why did everything feel so much smaller? How was memory capable of magnifying everything?

I looked at the building's sign and smiled. A Thai café had taken over. It felt right to go and order a tea. I entered the building and walked down the hall and accidentally passed the café. I caught the café cashier's grin as I backtracked and walked in.

I was wrong. The café hadn't taken the place of the chocolate shop; it took the place of the bookstore. I ordered my tea, thanked the cashier, and stepped back into the hallway.

To my left was a folding security gate, cordoning off what was once the chocolate shop. Hallway lights spilled halfway into the vacant unit. I walked up to the gate and scanned the area, reconstructing in my head all the decorations, counters, and tables. I let out a heavy sigh and left the building.

Instead of going to my car, I walked to the edge of the lot, leaned against its railing, and stared at the downtown area.

"There's symbolism here," I said out loud, the cold air sinking into my skin. "I don't think I can leave until it reveals itself."

The vacant unit made my heart hurt. The emptiness made something echo in my soul.

Sometimes change is morally neutral. Sometimes change is inevitable. Sometimes change is heavy, hard, necessary, and rough.

Sometimes things leave and new things take their place.

But sometimes it's not about seeing what will fill up the space left by what came before.

Sometimes it's about making peace with vacancy.

Sometimes whimsy is replaced with half-lit shadows, and the best you can do is hold the memories that made everything larger than life.

I know that the price of wisdom is lessons learned the hard way. We trade in innocence for the knowledge of good and evil—but

THE YEAR OF DATING MYSELF

innocence was what made it so easy for the snake to trick Eve in the first place.

The world still had whimsy. I still had whimsy. It just wasn't going to look like it did before.

I bid the building a farewell and started my drive home. For the first time in years, I intentionally played Christmas music. Bing Crosby eventually came on the radio, wishing me a merry little Christmas—reminding me that, until we can reunite, we have no choice but to muddle through. *Somehow.*

Chapter 48: Homecoming

I didn't know what to make of things as I drove into my hometown a second time. There was a quaint nostalgia to it all, the second time around. I wanted to stop by the library that had been a staple of my childhood to see if the old metal swings were still there. I knew the chances were slim, but I still wanted to check.

"Holy renovations, Batman," I said out loud as I turned the corner and the library came into view.

Only it wasn't just renovated. It was a completely different building. The new building was twice the size, with big, angular walls of glass on one side. It was sleek and modern, and it made my heart hurt. I didn't even have to walk to the back of the building to know that the old metal swings were a thing of the past. But I followed the path around and made note of the beautiful new landscaping and the intricately designed playground. The basketball court and mural had been replaced with a tiered garden. What had once felt like endless meadows as a kid had been replaced with luxury high-rises.

Sometimes things will take the place of what came before, and you will still have to make peace with vacancy.

THE YEAR OF DATING MYSELF

I drove to where my old high school had once been, knowing full well that the building had been demolished years prior. But I still felt disoriented, looking at what took its place. It was like the town was in a perpetual battle with what came before and what was yet to come.

My childhood neighborhood didn't catch my throat the way that it had in January. It played out before me like a familiar, melancholic song. I pulled up to my childhood home and rang the doorbell.

"Hey Sis," my brother said. His dog was at his side, tentatively wagging his tail at me.

"Hey!" I said. I gave the dog a gentle pat, turned, saw my mom, and reflexively added: "Hey Mom!"

"Oh, I recognize you!" My mom's face lit up. "It helps that you look like other family members."

I grinned sheepishly.

"So, what's the occasion?" she asked.

"Oh, just . . . wanted to visit," I said. "I meant to visit earlier."

"Let me show you what I've done with the house since you were last here," said my brother.

I followed him as he pointed out new window installations and new furniture. I walked with him down to the basement so he could show off the new dryer. Hampers of clothing and linens had taken the place of my boxes of childhood toys.

"Oh, don't mind those," said my brother. "When Mom gets incontinent multiple days in a row, laundry tends to back up."

I pressed my lips into a thin line, taking in the full scope of what caregiving for our mom entailed.

"How's everything been?" I asked, out of earshot of our mom.

"It's getting worse," he replied. "She's walked out of the house multiple times in the middle of the night. The police find her and bring her back."

"How much longer do you have on the waitlist?"

"About two more months."

My brother showed me a few other rooms. I didn't open and close cabinets, or remark on how small everything was, like the first time I visited. Instead, I noticed a set of shelves in one room that housed a few of my brother's old toys. One collection included a few toys that had been mine, but I kept that to myself. It was heartwarming to see how we both were doing what we could to memorialize the brighter parts of our childhood.

We stood at the top of the stairs on the second floor. On the first floor, our mom was watching TV and making non sequitur comments about the show. My brother and I inevitably started talking about our upbringing—like two survivors of a disaster, knowing the other is uniquely qualified to understand.

"I found a bunch of letters, when cleaning out Mom's desk," said my brother. "Grandma was paying for a lot of our groceries and toys when we were kids."

"I wondered, sometimes, how they were able to afford anything, given how much Dad drank," I said. "Now we know the answer is: they weren't."

"Yeah, drinking—and gambling," said my brother.

"Gambling?"

"Sports betting," he said. "He had a pretty bad gambling addiction. Grandma was helping Mom out a lot, behind the scenes."

I thought about my maternal grandma, about what must've been going through her mind as she helped her daughter buy food because her son-in-law had drunk and gambled away the money.

"Also, apparently Mom and Great Aunt Peggy had a falling out, at some point," my brother added.

My jaw dropped.

"What?"

THE YEAR OF DATING MYSELF

"I don't know what happened," he continued. "But *something* did, and they never really spoke to each other after that. I can read through the letters, see if I can find out why."

"So that's why Aunt Peggy seemingly vanished," I said. I thought about the crystals I'd grown from her kit and felt a weight in my chest.

I helped my brother as he cooked dinner. I looked at the two framed photos on the wall: the two mountaintop shots, one of my mom, one of my dad, from a time before children, a time before marriage. A time when it was just them and the mountains of New Hampshire. My dad, looking pensively off to the side in his photo. My mom, a large, beaming smile in hers. A mountain range in the distance that I recognized by sight. It was timeless and peaceful, and weighed down my soul.

We had dinner by the coffee table, just like before. I looked at my mom and thought about what it must've been like, trying to raise two children in such an environment. A stay-at-home mom with no income of her own, yet also responsible for finding the means to get food on the table. I thought about the Christmas mornings with all our toys under the tree. I thought about when my grandmother might've threatened to rewrite her will if my mom didn't divorce my father. How likely it might've been around the time when my grandmother was paying for our groceries.

Was that something my mom turned to her Aunt Peggy about, only for Aunt Peggy to agree with her sister?

What layered worlds adults have that children are completely oblivious to.

"Thanks for visiting. Seriously," said my brother, in a tone that revealed just how deep those words ran.

"Of course," I said. "I should visit more often."

I said my goodbyes and gave my mom a gentle hug. The woman who once towered over me barely reached my collarbone. I lingered in the hug, pausing in a moment that had no proper word for it.

I sat in my car, afterward, letting the interior lights fade to black. The visit, while heavy, was somehow easy. I was used to gut-wrenching, stressful visits. But it was okay. Enjoyable, even. What was the difference?

I initially shrugged off the question and put my key in the ignition. Before I could start my car, I had a realization so strong that it made me take my keys back out. The interior lights turned back on, illuminating me.

What was the difference? The difference was that, the times before, I was entering that house as the ghost of a younger me. I was the wounded child, the parentified child, the prodigal daughter. I was perennially the little kid, simultaneously desperate for her parents' love and protesting what had been done to her.

That was before I brought my toys home and truly mourned the childhood that I was given. That was before all the parts of me had started to meld, until I stopped being a fragmented collection of pain and became a more unified, multifaceted person.

It was the first time I'd walked into that house as an adult.

I thought about playing Peter, Paul, Mary on my drive home, like I had in January, but decided instead on Christmas music. As I drove through town, the colonial-era homes abutting new development neighborhoods, I sunk into my newfound revelation. I pulled up images in my mind of my childhood Christmases. I thought about that little girl in her pattern cotton PJs, staring up at the lights, mesmerized by the amazing world around her. Tears streamed down my face as I continued north. I wasn't sad or mournful. The emotions were just too heavy to react any other way.

Acknowledging that I was finally an adult meant truly taking in the passage of time, and I felt the growing pains in my bones.

THE YEAR OF DATING MYSELF

I skipped Frank Sinatra's version of "Have Yourself a Merry Little Christmas"—one that erases the line about muddling through. I skipped it for the same reason I skip any version of the song that speeds up the tempo or tries to put a jolly spin on it. The song is not meant to be *jolly*. It's a song that embraces melancholy. It's a song that dares to show how beautiful things are when they're given permission to sink.

Chapter 49: Investment

Investing in myself has given me one of the best returns on investment I've ever experienced.

I wrote that line in my final self-care entry for my class. I decided to reveal in the entry the reason I began the Year of Dating Myself. I gave it a short sentence—a quick blurb about leaving an abusive relationship and realizing my patterns—before shifting focus to what my journey had been like. I thought about what it would've looked like, had I revealed the reason at the beginning of the year. Half of the journal entry would've been about the abuse I'd gone through instead of what I was finally able to do.

At the beginning of the year, I was trying to invest in myself while still orbiting my pain. I knew why I did it. It was for the same reason a knee injury can become your entire world. You navigate life through the lens of your injury. There's no shame in something that large becoming the center of your universe.

But I was in a different place. My metaphorical knee was functional again. I could finally orbit myself.

I thought about that as I made use of Gabe's birthday present to me—a sushi making class, something for my Solo Tour—a few days after visiting my mom. I drove down to the Boston area for

THE YEAR OF DATING MYSELF

my class, stopping off at a mall to finally use a photo booth. It wasn't an old-fashioned booth but instead a modern, digital one, but the compromise was worth finally checking it off the list.

As I left the mall, I passed an indoor mini golf park, the area encased in blacklight with its decorations glowing vibrantly. I made a note to myself to return after the holiday season. Mini golf would make for a perfect solo date.

I found the sushi-making class, went inside, and found my seat. I conversed lightly with the couple who shared a table with me. While I was certain I was going to mess up, I was pleasantly surprised to find how easily I could make my own rolls.

I was also pleasantly surprised by how little I felt like the third wheel at the table. A part of me wondered if the couple felt obligated to talk with me because I was effectively by myself, but at no point did I feel like a charity case. I was there to learn a new skill. I had a wonderful time, and was entertained by our comedic chef.

I was finally the center of my own experience.

I thought about that as I saw my therapist the following week. I could feel how different our session was, how much of it was spent with me explaining the work I'd been able to do outside of her office. We'd already had a few sessions like it, and I could feel the rumble it was creating. So it was no surprise when she asked me where we went from "here."

"Now, this is entirely up to you," she said. "If you'd still prefer to meet regularly, we can definitely do that. Likewise, if anything ever comes up and we need to pick back up again, I'm only a phone call away. But what I'm seeing is someone who's been able to incorporate the work we've been doing into their everyday life. I see the adult version of you at the helm of your ship. I see those younger versions finally feeling safe enough to rest."

I nodded. I remembered that past version of me, the one who'd just gotten out of the disastrous situation with the man who had the hammock. She was realizing that she needed help—that she was developing a pattern, that it was time to go back to therapy and unpack why she kept doing it to herself.

There was a heartbreaking beauty in the parallel. Even that past version of me understood something needed to be done. She had zero clue what the next few years would have in store—that she would repeat that pattern two more times before she'd finally remove herself from the equation—but she'd be proud of the woman she became.

Heaven knows I was proud of her.

"No, I agree as well," I said. "It might be time to see what it's like with the training wheels off."

"The training wheels have been off for a while," countered my therapist. "You just no longer need my reassurance that you know how to bike."

I walked out of the office and felt the weight of closure on my shoulders. Past me had made the right decision in returning to therapy, the same way the version of me from nearly a year prior had made the right decision in dating herself.

The same way all those therapy sessions laid the foundation to build it, the Solo Tour had created a foundation for whatever would be built on top of it. What that was going to look like would only be revealed with time. I couldn't have predicted how the year would've gone, so why try predicting the future?

All I knew was that I was finally at the helm of my own ship. I was navigating the seas based not on what had happened to me, but where I wanted to go.

I had finally invested in myself, and the returns had been paying off in dividends.

Chapter 50: Light and Dark

"What are your plans for Christmas?" Lana asked.

I'd been careful with how I shared my Christmas plans. I knew, for some, if I led with, "I'll be alone for the first time," I'd immediately be given invitations by well-meaning people to join their Christmases—and my day was not a problem that needed to be solved.

"I'm actually going to be alone for the first time," I told Lana. "So, I'm going on a winter hike!"

"I think that's a great plan," said Lana, and started coming up with ways my trail food could pay homage to Christmas dinner. She gave me cranberry jam and fried onion toppers to assist in the Christmas trail food.

Now that's my idea of problem solving.

"There's something symbolic about a date like this on the winter solstice," I said to myself. "I just don't know what it means, yet."

On the winter solstice, the shortest day of the year, I had reservations at a candle-making place *and* a rage room. That alone tickled me. Two events on two opposite sides of the spectrum. The

THE YEAR OF DATING MYSELF

plan was to create my candle and, while it cooled, I'd walk the three city blocks over to the rage room. I'd then spend my hour in the room smashing and breaking—before returning to pick up my candle.

The rage room at Lana's bachelorette party was still fresh in my mind, even though it happened way back in March. It had been profoundly cathartic. I knew it would be good to let out any anger, one more time. There was a lot from that year that I wanted to leave behind, and I was going to do my best to facilitate that.

I walked into the candle shop, the assortment of aromas greeting me at the door. The owner walked me through how to choose my scents and mix the wax. It was a relatively short activity, but I loved what I'd made.

With a little extra time on my hands, I walked to a shop for local artists. One section housed ornate glass designs. I went through the collection until a crow ornament caught my eye. I smiled and immediately picked it up.

I never did get to befriend my murder of crows, but it was a decent consolation prize.

I dropped off my new ornament in my car and made my way to the rage room. I changed into my jumpsuit, filled my crate with breakables, and eyed the appliances—which I could add on, for an additional fee.

"Could I get the toaster oven?" I asked the rage room employee, as if I were shopping at Sears.

I put on my helmet and pulled out my first item: a mug with "Let It Be" in tiny print across it.

In another life, I would've purchased such a mug, but that day it felt right to kickstart my time by throwing it on the ground, the ceramic shattering into countless pieces.

I threw plates against the wall. I took a sledgehammer to the toaster oven.

"This is for everything that pissed me off this year!" I shouted and smashed a glass.

I gave myself permission to think of everything that made me seethe. I thought about tactics and antics and things that never saw proper comeuppance. I dug up things my ex had said to me—things that people I thought were friends had said to me, things that strangers online had said, both to me and about me. I shoved them to the front of my mind as I took a crowbar to a thick glass vase.

I eventually ran out of things to break. The toaster oven was a crumpled mess. I technically still had another half hour in the rage room, but I knew it was time. I scanned the room, taking slow breaths. I looked down and saw a fragment of the first mug I'd shattered.

In the center of the fragment was one word:

"Be."

I exited the room, changed out of my jumpsuit, and went to pick up my candle.

A part of me was mildly disappointed. The rage room, while fun, didn't provide the same cathartic release as the first one had.

But another part of me was reassured by that realization.

Of course it was different! I didn't get extreme release—but that was because I didn't need it. Catharsis can only be as large as what's been held in. It was a *good* thing that I didn't need the same release. I couldn't imagine still having the same level of hurt and anger as I had in March.

Sometimes you don't realize how much you've already let go until you try to put it down.

I picked up my candle and returned to my car. I sat in my driver's seat, thinking about the winter solstice. The winter solstice is the darkest day of the year. It's a reminder that darkness is an inevitable part of life, and that the world exists in cycles of birth and death.

It's also a day to celebrate—because it reminds us that brighter days are ahead.

On the shortest, darkest day of the year, I had both created my own light and leaned into my own darkness. And in that leaning in, I was reassured that each new day would be brighter than the last.

There was my symbolism, after all.

I woke up on Christmas Eve and knew that I was sick.

My muscles ached, my sinuses were raw, and my throat hurt so much it felt like I was swallowing glass. I spent the morning hoping it would fade, only to feel worse by the afternoon. There was no denying it. I was sick, and the kind of sick that doesn't disappear after a good night's rest. I tested for COVID-19 and it came back negative.

Thank the Lord for little favors, I guess.

"I'm trying not to throw a pity party for myself, but it's hard not to," I told Britt. "Because of course this had to happen." I paused and added: "I couldn't have any major event go right for me, this year. I'm just realizing that."

I felt my voice waver. I coughed and changed the subject.

I slogged to my kitchen and made myself soup. I put the kettle on for tea and I slumped against the counter. The brain fog was getting worse. My breathing was labored.

"If it's this bad tomorrow, I'll go to urgent care," I said to myself, wincing as I tried to slurp down my soup.

I walked up the stairs and into the bathroom. I opened my mouth wide in the mirror and tried to peer down my throat. No white spots; most likely not strep throat then.

Thank the Lord for more little favors.

I guess.

I lit the candles around my bathtub, turned on the water, and dumped bubble bath solution into the tub. Why did I turn to bubble baths only in times of crisis? I'd meant to make baths a regular occurrence. I'd done only two in the beginning of the year before abandoning the practice.

As the water ran, I sat down on my bed, put my head in my hands, and cried. I didn't want to be the host of the pity party, but sometimes you don't get to be the event planner. So much of the Solo Tour had been compromised, and they were never small hiccups. I thought about getting pulled over before Valentine's Day. I thought about catching COVID at Pride. I thought about watching my birthday weekend get taken away from me. I thought about every plan I had to cancel during the summer because I kept getting sick. And there I was, sick *again*. Instead of celebrating solitude on Christmas, I was just going to be sick—with no one around, and not an open store in sight.

The logical side of me knew that I was catastrophizing—that plenty of events had gone off without a hitch. But logic and emotions still sat on opposite sides of the chasm during cataclysms like that. I stared with bleary eyes at my bathtub, the candles giving everything an ethereal glow.

I stopped trying to make logic bridge the gap. Instead, I closed my eyes and asked, "What is it about things going wrong this year that hurts so much?"

I handed the mic over to my emotions and asked them to speak their peace.

Underneath the frenzied sadness, the fury that *nothing could go right*, the tantruming declaration that I might as well cancel Québec City, was a whisper of truth:

It felt like I was being told that I wasn't allowed to heal.

At the root of it all was a nagging feeling like I didn't have permission to pick up the pieces—let alone rebuild. It was the echoes of people who'd always preferred my spirit broken. The family members who were outraged that I spoke candidly about my father. The friends who stopped being friends because I talked about the abuse from my last relationship. The predators and perpetrators who preferred me meek, who wanted me in a holding pattern—because to heal would mean to wise up. Even my patient zero always seemed to come back into my life right as I started to move on.

Let me be. Let me heal, I'd silently plead before agreeing to meet him for coffee.

The scales in my life felt unbalanced—and every upended plan felt like being chastised for trying to equal them out. The more weight we give to an event, the more devastating its collapse.

I watched the bubbles peek above the bathtub's rim. I got up, turned off the water, and got ready for my bath.

I leaned my head against the tub and breathed. I wasn't going to cancel Québec City, even though I was convinced *something* was going to happen to ruin the trip. The only thing I could do was hope that I recovered in time for it.

I looked over and saw two familiar sights, leaning against the tiles by the edge of the bathtub. I smiled, sat up, and reached for them.

By the edge of my tub sat my toy turtle and rubber ducky. They were once staples of my childhood baths. I held each tenderly as I added them to my bath. The rubber duck bobbled. The turtle went vertical, its little head popping up, looking as if it were treading water. The ducky was smudged with dirt and the turtle's color had faded, but both were in good shape. I watched them navigate the water and felt something heavy and beautiful in my chest.

So much had gone wrong that year, but the one thing that had gone undeniably *right* was the return to my childhood home. I'd brought back my childhood toys. I'd taken the time to cherish the relics of my younger years. I'd healed the wounded child side of me.

Perhaps even more than healing my romantic wounds, healing that part of me was the most important thing that I'd done. It was a chance to ask, "How did I get here?" from a positive point of view. Look at all the progress that I'd made. Look at the person I finally got to become. The journey was flawed, but it still progressed forward.

I'm so tired. But I can still do this.

Eventually the water became tepid. I got out and opened the drain. As the water slowly disappeared, I scooped out my duckie and my turtle, gave them both a kiss, and sat them back down at the edge of the tub.

I woke up Christmas morning in a fog, but also on the mend.

My throat, while still raw, felt a thousand times better. My muscles still ached and my energy was still low, but I was better than the day before. I looked outside. The weather was misty and gray, with a thick fog rolling through the trees. Even if I'd been healthy, I probably would've scrapped the hike—but without any of the revelations that I had on Christmas Eve.

When everything goes wrong, everything else has to go right to get you where you need to be.

I sat at my kitchen table, where I'd stacked a few gifts from friends. I started with the gift that Gabe had dropped off before he flew out to see his family for the holidays.

I peeled back the wrapping paper, let out the loudest laugh, and felt the tears rim my eyes.

THE YEAR OF DATING MYSELF

Underneath the wrapping paper was a crystal growing kit.

It was the modern version of what Aunt Peggy had gotten me. It boasted glow in the dark crystals. If my bathtub toys were a reminder of how far I've come, the new crystal kit was a reminder that the journey was still ongoing.

That moment was more important than any hike could've been.

Chapter 51: Layers

I took it easy for the remainder of the week. By the end, I was left with a raspy voice that demanded rest. I hated that—once again—I was without a voice. But I tried my best to focus on the positive: at least I was healthy enough to drive to Québec City.

"Plus, all the vocal rest will mean even more introspection than I already was doing," I said to Britt before dissolving into a coughing fit, my throat making sure the punishment for talking was direct and swift.

The introspection was already in abundance. In my silent packing, I realized that my return to Québec had an additional layer to it: Québec, the province, was also the first vacation I'd ever planned by myself.

Nearly a decade before—and barely a year before everything fell apart—I had planned a trip to Montreal with Gabe. It was the first time I'd ever planned a trip for us. I'd made every rookie mistake, and instead of taking it as a learning experience, I took it as proof that I'm incapable and that I should never try things on my own.

The same way that the Solo Tour had become far more than healing from an abusive relationship, my return to Québec was proving the same.

THE YEAR OF DATING MYSELF

I set off for the Canadian border, listening to songs but unable to sing along to them. I felt something stir within me, something that needed to be released, one way or another. I turned to a song that was guaranteed to make me cry.

Sometimes catharsis comes from whatever it'll take to light the fuse.

I started playing a song about Scotland—a song that referred to the country by its Latin name of Caledonia. The tears immediately formed. There was something tender and raw about the song. You could feel the homesickness in the words. I was only a few miles from the Canadian border when I thought to myself: *I want to visit Scotland.*

I want to visit Scotland. I want to return to my roots.

My father's side of the family was Irish, but my mother's side was Scottish. When my marriage ended, I almost opted to change my last name to MacGregor—my maternal grandmother's maiden name. So much of my mother's lineage was lost to the sands of time, but I wanted to retrace my ancestors' footsteps.

I turned off the song as I got in line at the border crossing. Who knew what would happen if the border agent saw me crying?

I got into Canada with little issue and continued the second half of my journey. The day turned into night as I pulled into a parking spot and made my way up to the apartment I was renting.

The first order of business was food. After changing out of my driving clothes, I walked over to Old Québec.

During my first trip there, I'd found every excuse to pass on a restaurant.

"This one isn't it. I need to find a place that's just right," I'd tell myself until every restaurant was closed.

But that day, I stepped into the first restaurant that caught my eye.

The restaurant was beautiful but busy. I gave a shaky, "bonsoir," to the host, who immediately started speaking to me in English.

"How long is the wait for one person?" I asked in my raspy voice. A once-impossible task, easily accomplished. What an act of triumph it is when our mountains shrink to molehills.

"For one? We can serve you now," he said.

I sat down at my seat and knew exactly what I was going to get—because it was the one thing I'd feverishly wanted on my first trip, and then never got.

"I'll have a classic poutine," I told the waitress.

I walked past an outdoor ice-skating rink after dinner and prayed that my ice skates were still in the back of my car. I strolled around Old Québec, feeling like I'd returned home. The streets were alive with lights and music and people. I could feel something settle in my bones.

I'm meant to be here for New Year's. This is exactly where I'm supposed to be.

I started walking out of Old Québec and toward the music festival happening just outside of it. I danced contently with myself as the DJ played. Around me were families, couples, groups of friends—but I could see a few individuals, also there to enjoy things alone like me. I felt the beaming smile wash over my face.

I called it early that night. I knew how precarious my health was, and I had no plans of getting sick again, just in time for New Year's. I started walking back to my apartment. As the music faded behind me, a memory of my father took its place in my mind.

It was an evening where my mother's episode had upended the entire night. The dust had settled, but it left everything feeling grimy. My father, already drunk but in a tender moment of *in vino veritas*, had tried to explain my mother's aggressiveness toward me.

"You've got the same personality as her mother, your grandmother," he'd said. "You're just as strong-willed as her. That's why your mother gets so mad at you."

I stopped midstride on the sidewalk. *Was Caledonia calling out to me because of this? Did I inherit my grandmother's spirit?*

No wonder, then, that my mom felt so compelled to break it.

I detoured to my car and opened my trunk. There, in an oversized bag, were my ice skates.

How gently things can come full circle.

I let the chill of the night stir in my heart as I went inside, changed into my PJs, and crawled into bed.

"Geez, the Québecois are even faster than Bostonians."

I kept getting passed as I walked through Old Québec the next morning. I had a few things on the docket for the day: I wanted to go ice-skating, I wanted to visit Lower Town, and I wanted to enjoy another night of the musical festival. But otherwise, I had an open schedule.

That was what I wanted. The same way I'd once charged through hiking trails, I'd once overcharged my travel itineraries. It was a chance to slow it down.

And that's what I did. I strolled through Lower Town, stopping to watch an acrobatic show: four henchmen in neon ski masks trying to steal the contortionist's Christmas gift. Eventually, the henchmen were successful and started running down the street, tossing the gift in the air and urging the audience to follow them. I followed the crowd as the henchmen stopped at a trampoline, continuing the skit, teasing each other with the present as they did jumping tricks.

I returned to the apartment, grabbed my ice skates, and went skating. The ice rink was crowded and with little room for tricks, but I still added in a few crossovers as I made my turns.

My first ice-skating dates had unlocked my guilt about the end of my marriage—guilt that probably influenced dating *after* my marriage, if I was being honest with myself. Yes, patient zero was why I'd frantically *started* dating—but had my repressed guilt acted like the ghost of Christmas past? Did it work in tandem with all my childhood wounds?

Our motivations are wild and layered and complicated. There is never just one angle.

I used the afternoon for rest—something a previous version of myself would've never been okay with. *How can I rest, when I only have so much time in this city?*

Back then, I was able to ignore my fatigue. But the new me not only noticed it, she knew how to respect it.

"It's because I'm out of survival mode," I told myself.

It was undeniable. When my default mode was survival, I didn't give myself the chance to feel tired. Everything had to run on all cylinders, all the time.

I was tired, but I could finally rest because I didn't have to fight or play that game anymore.

When I set out for the music festival that night, a family passed me by, speaking to each other in singsongy Spanish. I almost smacked my head with the realization.

I was surrounded by tourists—and I'd never, not once, been out-paced by a tourist before.

These weren't naturally faster walkers.

I was just strolling.

I was finally savoring an experience, instead of charging to the next thing.

THE YEAR OF DATING MYSELF

I stayed at the festival for a few songs before deciding that particular DJ wasn't for me. Such an easy conclusion added an important second part to my realization: being out of survival mode also meant that I was no longer leaning on the good things like my survival depended on it.

God knows I'd leaned on so many of my Solo Tour stops as if my very survival were on the line.

It was undeniably a reason why I'd become devastated when plans went awry. I'd never know for sure what my reaction would've been to things like my birthday or getting pulled over before Valentine's Day, had I not been treating the events as my sole source of salvation. Removing one variable renders the entire equation invalid. It does me a disservice to think I can extricate one element of survival mode without it getting tangled up in the others.

But what I knew, then, was that life's beauty flourished more readily when not clung to.

I strolled away from the festivities, the bass of the music still permeating the air as I returned to my neighborhood. I was a few feet from my apartment building when a man approached me, speaking French with a nervous smile on his face.

"Oh, *je suis désolé . . .*" I attempted to stammer out an apology for not speaking French. My pronunciation was enough for the man to pause, grin, and switch to English.

"Ah, you're visiting!" he said. "I was just saying that I find you very beautiful. Perhaps . . . you would like to stay in touch?"

"Oh," I replied. "I'm engaged."

"Oh, that's okay! That's okay! I hope you have a good evening!" he said. "*Bonsoir!*"

"*Bonsoir,*" I responded.

I barely knew French, but I knew he was originally trying to ask me out. Once he realized I was a tourist, he changed the request to a simple keeping in touch.

It was too on the nose, to be asked out in the final days of the Year of Dating Myself.

Life is poetry, even when some of the lines are clichéd.

However, as he walked away, I deliberately walked past my apartment. I circled the block before returning.

My rationale for the detour put a sobering twang to the experience. Had I entered the apartment building after our interaction, he would've seen where I was staying. He'd been kind—but there was no guarantee that a rejected man wouldn't return, after having some time to "think." History is filled with women who paid with their lives for turning down a man. I'd had my own share of frightening experiences in that department.

"Are you protecting yourself from romantic love?" the documentarian had asked.

Maybe. Maybe not. But sometimes I just need to protect myself from the reality of the world I live in.

Chapter 52: Bigger than Me

New Year's Eve. The last day.

I could feel the heaviness as I got ready.

A pretty profound chapter was closing. Something that started as an impulse ticket purchase from a promotional email had ignited a revolution within me. What felt like a manic dream from a woman still trying to pick up the pieces became one of the most transformative things I'd ever done.

"I've made a lot of bad dating decisions in the past," I told Britt. "But the decision to date myself is not one of them."

I made my way to the Citadelle of Québec and stared out at Old Québec. I'd known that specific vista for years, long before I ever visited.

A year or two after I visited Montreal, I received a brochure in the mail from Canada's travel bureau. The front showed Fairmont Le Château Frontenac from the vantage point of the Citadelle, stone-layered homes between the green hills and the chateau.

Want a Trip to Europe?, it asked in bold, white letters. I'd put the brochure on my fridge, wondering when I could go, but feeling like it was a pipedream.

THE YEAR OF DATING MYSELF

I'd return to that brochure, years later. I was ten months into—and, unbeknownst to me, three weeks from leaving—an abusive relationship. Instead of devoting Labor Day weekend to seeing my long-distance boyfriend, I'd opted to go on my first solo vacation and finally visit Québec City, a taste of Europe on the American continent.

It wasn't lost on me that the drive to Québec City was exactly as long as the drive to my then-boyfriend's place—but in the opposite direction.

An email might've sparked my Solo Tour, but a brochure had created the fuse, nearly a decade before. Sometimes I'm overwhelmed at the magnitude of the butterfly effect.

I took the long way back to Old Québec and passed by a group of people walking in the opposite direction, wearing keffiyehs and carrying the Palestinian flag. I gave a gentle, supportive nod. While I'd been busy with my solo dates, civilians in Gaza were dying en masse. The Israeli military had systematically bombed building after building, neighborhood after neighborhood. The world was crying for a ceasefire.

"No one's free until we're all free," I said aloud, my heart heavy.

How silly all my adventures felt at that moment.

I tried to refocus. I walked into Old Québec. I found a set of metal swings. The metal swings of my childhood were gone, but I'd found at least one set. I chose a swing and pumped my legs until I was parallel with the ground.

In a world filled with cruelty, childlike joys are sometimes what keeps us from completely collapsing.

I left the swing set and started walking back, ready to return to my apartment and get some rest. I turned a corner and heard the chanting. Police officers lined the streets, preparing for protesters as they started to march down the road. The people in front carried a black banner with *Palestine libre* painted in white.

I bit the inside of my cheek and focused on the pain to keep myself from crying. There was something so overwhelming and so heart-wrenching about what I was witnessing. I stayed in my spot on the sidewalk, standing in solidarity as the protesters passed. A woman called out chants in French and the crowd behind her repeated her call.

I had every intention to stand, bear witness, and then go home. But as the last protesters passed me, I turned and began walking with them.

I knew it wasn't a smart move to impulsively join a protest with zero preparations. I had friends back in the States who'd been tear gassed and assaulted for standing up for what was right. I had no safeguards if something went awry. But my heart wouldn't let me do anything else.

It's in those type of moments that perspective is delivered in deafening tones. The world is filled with unspeakable injustices, and the only thing we can do is fight—even if it feels like a losing battle, even if the scales will never be fully balanced. I watched people in restaurants give peace signs as the protestors walked past. Others applauded. I let the tears roll down my cheeks.

Me and my silly woes. There were mothers trying to dig their children out from rubble, half a world away. It's easy to dismiss our pain in light of world events. I tried my best to remember the balance—to recognize the privilege I'd been given, to have the luxury of rebuilding. I needed to remember that I shouldn't dismiss my own pain, but that my obligation to heal extended beyond my own little world.

Heal. Grow stronger. Grow wiser. Then use it to help make the world a better place.

The protest turned into an assembly by Fairmont Le Château Frontenac. I stood for a while, listening to words I didn't know, but understood the meaning to. Eventually, I returned to my apartment and collapsed onto my bed.

A part of me had lost motivation to finish the day, but I got myself up and out for one last dinner.

There'd been countless restaurants that I'd bookmarked for my first trip to Québec but never went to. It only felt right that my last dinner in Québec City was at one of those places.

I walked into the restaurant and asked if they had any space for one.

"Yes, we do," the host said and brought me over to a spot by the bar.

A little while later, the host sat a woman a few seats down from me. She was somewhere in her sixties and took her seat as if she owned it. Out of the corner of my eye, I caught the woman looking at me. I instinctively looked over. She gave me a warm, knowing smile and returned to her menu. Perhaps she, too, had learned to embrace the joy in taking herself out. Perhaps she could tell that I was doing the same. Perhaps the smile she gave me hinted that she was glad I'd figured it out at my age instead of hers.

Or, perhaps I was reading too much into it.

I decided to get dessert. I rarely did, but it was New Year's Eve, after all. I opened the menu one more time and scanned the desserts.

It was my turn to smile a knowing smile.

The first item on the list was crème brûlée.

If ever there was a dessert to have, after my birthday fiasco. I ordered my crème brûlée and indulged, *my* spoon breaking the caramelized surface. I slowly finished my dessert, savoring each bite, knowing no one was going to lay a hand on it.

I stepped into the frigid night and made my way to the New Year's Eve festival. The world around me was alive with people just as bundled up as me. I wandered with the crowds from one concert stage to the next. I settled on one spot and watched the area become packed with people.

There was an ache in me as I looked around. While I didn't see many couples, I saw countless groups of friends. I watched as they took pictures together, as they waved one another over. The feeling intensified as my phone started to buzz.

"I won't make it to midnight, so I want to say Happy New Year, my love," Lana texted. "It's an honor to call you my best friend and my platonic life mate."

"*Ay, querida*," I replied. "And a Happy New Year to you too! It was an honor to get to spend this year by your side!"

I was grateful to be back in Québec City. I was supposed to be there—and supposed to be there *alone*. But I longed to be celebrating with my friends.

What is life, without people to share it with?

There's a balance to things. I needed time alone to fortify myself. I needed to remember that my own company is worth keeping. But the fruits of my labor were never meant to be hoarded by myself.

It was to learn I could share my life with others, instead of just handing it over.

I felt the weight of the year's final hour. The Italian DJ hyped up the crowd in broken English. I'd been so focused on the year that it was disorienting to think about its end. I knew there would be life after the year, but seeing the banners that bid it farewell was jarring.

In just minutes, another year would begin. A chance to take what that year had given me and pay it forward. The Year of Dating Myself was almost over, but in many ways it'd just begun.

THE YEAR OF DATING MYSELF

The LED screens that lit up the city square switched to the final countdown. The crowd chanted in equal parts French and English. I watched the numbers dwindle down, feeling a bittersweet pang, like wishing a beloved well before they set off on a journey of their own.

"Three, two, one!" I heard the English parts of the crowd.

"*Bonne année!*" the LED displayed, before the words divided in triplicate and danced around the screen. All I could hear from the crowd was cheering. Fireworks went off by the walls of Old Québec. The DJ started playing ABBA's "Gimme! Gimme! Gimme! (A Man After Midnight)" and the whole crowd erupted.

We all jumped to the music, momentarily one single entity celebrating a new beginning.

Happy New Year.

Part XIII:
January (the following year)

Epilogue: What Now?

I woke up the next morning and began packing my things. I'd only rented the apartment for four days, and yet it felt like I was an undergrad again, moving out of my dorm.

An era was over. Time to go home.

I took one last stroll around Old Québec. The streets were empty. The stages for the New Year's Eve festival were already being dismantled. I passed by one woman on the sidewalk, who paused her phone conversation to say, "*Bonne année!*"

"*Bonne année,*" I croaked out. Being in the city with barely a voice had made it that much harder to communicate, but I noticed how I was already finding more ease in French. I said little more than greetings and apologies, but just a few days in a French-speaking town had shifted things for a person who spoke zero French. It made me think about how "*improve my Spanish,*" had been on my list for the Year of Dating Myself. Spanish—a language I'd once built up—was rapidly fading. I'd wanted to use the Year of Dating Myself to gain some of my proficiency back.

The goal sat on the list unchecked.

"I'll just have to spend time in a Spanish-speaking country," I told myself.

THE YEAR OF DATING MYSELF

I started driving home. I knew I could've stayed for longer—I didn't even have to pass in my apartment keys until noon—but I was ready to get back.

I felt the swell of the new year as I got back onto the highway and made my way south. The sun peaked out from the clouds as it began to snow. The snowflakes were so light that they floated through the air, giving the world a snow globe feel.

A question that had been dancing in the periphery was at the forefront: *What now?*

It was a specific and pointed question. Answering it with solo adventures wasn't going to cut it. The question wanted to know about romance.

Was I planning to stay single?

The answer was complicated. A part of me was open to it. If the right person came along—if the circumstances were right—I *might* be willing. But I thought about my plans for the year. My spring semester was about to start. It would be my last academic semester before I started my fieldwork. I still had my 4.0 GPA—and I wasn't about to lose it in the last semester. I was set to visit Danielle in February, and Britt in March. Britt and I had also just confirmed our trip to Greece, and I was eyeing a detour through Switzerland before returning to the States—and, thanks to my revelation during my New Year's trip, I wondered how much it would cost to get to Scotland from Switzerland.

I thought about how much I already had on my plate. Between work, school, friends, and solo adventures, I had no idea where romance would even fit in. If I were going to invite romance into my life, it would have to be worth it—the kind that enhanced my life, because I had no space for detractions.

As it *should* be.

I'd recently received two promotional emails: one from my favorite band, informing me that they were returning in March, and one from the candlelight concerts, informing me that they were returning in February. I bought a solo ticket for both.

Little moments of redemption and coming full circle.

A few hours into my drive, Georgia sent a message with a picture of the two of us, bathing in a gorgeous hot spring on New Year's Day.

"Can you believe that was *only* a year ago?" Georgia remarked. "Happy New Year my darling!"

I replied, calling Georgia *"querida"*—roughly translated from Spanish as "cherished one"—like I had with Lana. I'd once reserved the pet name for romantic partners, but I enjoyed using it for my beloved friends as well.

"It genuinely feels like a lifetime ago!" I said in my reply, before asking her about her New Year's trip with her new boyfriend.

I made it to the border crossing and waited in line. I remembered how I felt, the last time I was there—like I was waiting for the executioner. But instead, I entertained myself by going through the photos and videos I had taken on New Year's Eve.

"Where did you go in Canada?" the border agent asked.

"Québec City," I answered.

"Friends? Family?"

"I just love the city."

The agent handed my passport back to me and I continued toward Vermont. I put on the song about Caledonia one more time and found it pinging differently than before.

Yes, someday I'll visit Scotland. I'll take the time to feel where my ancestral roots lay.

Caledonia was, in fact, calling me.

But, at that moment, I was going home. *My* home.

I wanted to know my ancestral roots—but I'd also been laying down my own roots, in my own soil.

THE YEAR OF DATING MYSELF

As the song ended, I passed the exit sign for Caledonia Airport. Life is poetry. Pay attention when the lines start rhyming.

I drove across Vermont and into New Hampshire, greeting the mountains I knew well. Fresh snow had fallen, giving Franconia Notch an ethereal feel. I couldn't wait to get home and write out what I wanted to do for the new year.

The Year of Dating Myself was over, but that didn't mean I couldn't have another Solo Tour.

I continued south. I was twenty minutes from my house when my phone started ringing, with Gabe on the other line.

"Hello!" I responded jovially.

"Hey, uh, I know you're still on the road but, uh . . ." Gabe's voice was clipped. "I just got back from Boston and . . . I found Salem lying on my kitchen floor. He can't move his hind legs. I'm bringing him to the emergency hospital now."

My heart sank. I prayed it was nothing. I thanked Gabe for telling me and asked him to keep me updated. I got home and nothing felt real. I sat down, tried to make my new Solo Tour list, but found no motivation.

Half an hour later, Gabe called again.

"It's . . . bad," he said. "They think it was a stroke. His potassium levels are low. They can't get his body temperature up. I . . . I think you might want to come down here."

I grabbed my coat and got into my car. Tears blurred my vision as I sped down the highway, weaving through lanes. The highway signs as I crossed into Massachusetts read: Be Safe on New Year's. Don't Drive Impaired.

I got to the same hospital where Salem had once received his chemotherapy. I tried to calm myself down before I reached the front door and failed miserably. My crying made the hoarseness in my throat worse, making it impossible to speak.

"Salem," was the only coherent word I said.

320

The front desk woman immediately got up and brought me back to an exam room, where Gabe was waiting. He offered a hug and I stepped into it, shaking.

"The vet on staff tonight is recommending we put him down," said Gabe. "I told them like hell if we're doing that."

Gabe had already signed off on treatment to get Salem's potassium levels and body temperature raised. When the vet came in to get permission for any additional measures that might be needed that night, Gabe answered, "Without a doubt, and that includes extraordinary measures. Whatever it takes."

Whatever it takes. Don't let my baby die.

They gave us a chance to visit Salem in the intensive care unit. He was wrapped in a heated blanket, with IVs in his front paws. He was mildly sedated but perked up when he saw us.

"This is no way for the two-time champion against cancer to defend his belt," I whispered, my forehead against his, my tears soaking his fur.

"We'll keep you updated on his status," said one of the veterinary techs.

I kept my eyes on the ground, wishing I could disappear.

Britt called me on my drive back from the hospital and held space for me as I wept.

"This was the worst time for this to happen," I cried. "The one time—the one time—no one was around to look after Salem, and he collapses. It's not fair!"

"It's okay to feel this way," said Britt. "It isn't fair! The timing was terrible. It's also okay to be upset about the timing, for your sake too. You didn't even get a chance to come home from your trip before the rug was pulled out from you."

"I needed to hear that," I told her. "I really did. I've been feeling so selfish that a part of me is angry that, once again, something had to get taken away. I'm not allowed to just have a win."

THE YEAR OF DATING MYSELF

I felt all my repressed fury bubble to the surface. I was at my boiling point. I had *just* found the silver lining in canceling my Christmas, in spending the week sick, in having laryngitis yet again for New Year's.

I'd just found peace in upended plans.

I'd kicked and scratched and clawed my way into healing, despite setback after setback—and there I was, my temples pulsating from crying, my heart shattered across Interstate 93.

What was the point of it all, then?

It felt like the more I fought for something good, the bigger the gut punch ended up being. I thought about Salem's cancer journey. He'd fought through two rounds of chemo. Two rounds. Both times, we thought the cancer was gone for good. Both times, all signs pointed to him finally getting better.

Only for that to happen.

I thought about all the protesting, and how so much of it seemed to fall on deaf ears. How much of a lie it was, the idea that the moral arc of the world ultimately bends toward justice. This planet—this dying planet, this rapidly dying planet—was home to eons of cyclical fights for equality and freedom, only for humans to collectively never learn from the past and repeat the same mistakes.

What was the *fucking* point?

It all felt so trivial, so pointless. What was the point of progressing forward when failure was inevitable?

"I think I'm going to give up now," I said to Britt.

I thought about my clinical psychology degree that I was one semester away from doing my fieldwork in. I tried for some macabre comedic relief, imagining a despairing client, overwhelmed with how bleak everything felt, only for me to say, "Nah, I'm right there with you. This is all meaningless."

The macabre comedy gave zero relief.

In some ways, I was the client. The kind of client that, if a therapist were hearing what I was saying to my friends, they'd be assessing for suicide risk. I started reassuring my friends like I was trying to convince them not to put me on a seventy-two-hour hold.

No, no, I have no intent. I have no plans.

I'm just so *tired*. I don't see the point of doing this anymore.

The Year of Dating Myself began to feel like rearranging deck chairs on the Titanic. *All of it* felt like that. The wind was out of my sails, and it wasn't going to stop the ship from crashing into the iceberg.

Gabe and I visited Salem the next day. We met with the specialist. Gabe talked as I studied the art on the wall to keep from breaking down.

Salem's cancer had returned. There was a chance it had metastasized to his spine. That was our best-case scenario.

"You know it's bad when you're *hoping* it's lymphoma," Gabe tried to joke. If it wasn't spinal lymphoma, then it meant he'd sustained neurological damage, and we had a bigger problem on our hands.

Too much was still up in the air. They were treating him across the board for everything. Decision trees fractalled out in our heads. What to do if the treatments didn't work. What to do if he couldn't use his hind legs anymore. The only thing we knew for certain was that he wasn't going to die in the hospital. Everything else was excruciatingly ambiguous.

"We'll have a better idea tomorrow," said the specialist. Unlike the emergency room vet, who kept telling us the treatments wouldn't work, that our best bet was euthanasia, the specialist was optimistic.

"If you want me to go at it full force—all gas, no brakes—then that's what I'll do," she said.

"All gas, no breaks," said Gabe.

"That's all I need to hear."

Gabe and I spent the evening trying to keep each other afloat. We realized we hadn't eaten in twenty-four hours and ordered a pizza. We tried to watch a comedian, but I started crying halfway through.

"I want to just get a bottle of wine," I said out loud, regretting my decision to no longer keep alcohol in my house.

"That's a bad idea," said Gabe, who didn't drink at all.

I needed to hear him say that. Had I been home alone, I would've already been on my way to the store.

"I feel like I've lost the plot," I admitted, the comedy special still on pause. "This is . . . past depression, I think. I just don't want to try anymore. It just feels . . . pointless. Like rearranging deck chairs on the Titanic."

"The best revenge is a life well lived," Gabe said after a moment. "And that includes revenge against the cruelty of life. In a world designed to make me want to give up, the last thing I'm going to do is give it what it wants."

"Pure spite as a motivator," I replied, and couldn't help but smirk.

We tried to start the show again and failed.

"I'm not ready," I choked out between sobs. "I'm not ready to say goodbye."

We started going through our phones, finding every picture and video we had of Salem. We reminisced on his hijinks. We replayed memories until our cheeks that were originally puffed out from crying were sore from smiling.

Salem's original prognosis, when they first found the tumor in his stomach, was two weeks. *Two weeks.* With chemo, he would have had a few months.

That had been years ago. Years.

The specialist had assumed there'd been a typo on his chart. Cats with lymphoma are not supposed to live that long. He hadn't completely beaten cancer, but he had completely beaten the odds. All his treatments—all that work—meant we had hours more footage and hundreds more photos and countless more memories.

We never finished watching that comedian. But we did find some way to laugh.

"I realized something," Gabe said, before we called it a night. "We keep saying it was the worst possible timing when Salem collapsed. It was the one night when neither of us could look after him. But what if it was the best possible timing?"

"How so?"

"If he'd collapsed under either of our watches, we would've assumed it was from arthritis," said Gabe. "We'd pick him up, put him on a cat bed. Maybe we'd call the vet—but it would've been our local vet."

I grimaced. I loved our local vet, but they were the same people who took four months and four separate visits before they finally did an ultrasound on Salem and found the tumor.

"It was also New Year's Day," Gabe continued. "Only emergency hospitals were going to be open, which included the one with some of the best vets in the country, with some of the only specialists around, with the most advanced technology.

"When I found him on the kitchen floor, I knew it was an emergency. He was on death's door when I got to Mass Vet. They were the only people who could've saved him."

"Twelve hours earlier or twelve hours later, one of us would've been there for him, but he also might've died," I finished the thought.

When everything goes wrong, everything else has to go right.

I felt my raging fury dwindle to smoke.

The specialist called the next morning. Treatment was working better than they could've ever imagined.

"It's a night and day difference," she said.

We weren't completely out of the woods. We'd need to meet with oncology to figure out what to do next, to find the balance between maximizing survival but also quality of life.

But he was walking again. He was eating.

And he could finally come home.

Gabe and his girlfriend met me at the hospital, a peculiar trio as we went through the discharge papers with the veterinary tech. Salem was going to need multiple medications, every day. He needed to stay away from stairs and high places.

But he was going home.

Salem was exhausted and disoriented but too excited to rest. I watched over Salem while Gabe and his girlfriend finished building a ramp so Salem could walk up onto Gabe's bed. Logistically, it was going to be a nightmare. Salem was going to need around the clock supervision and care. The days of both Gabe and I being out of town at the same time were a thing of the past. All that, while knowing that Salem's time was limited. Odds were high that we'd lose him before the year was out.

But that didn't mean we'd stop trying. If anything, it was a reminder to cherish the time we had left.

I kept coming back to the image of rearranging deck chairs on the Titanic—my go-to metaphor for the futility of it all, the creeping dread that I'm just biding my time before the inescapable icy abyss. Maybe I was on the metaphorical deck of the Titanic, but I wasn't there to rearrange the furniture.

I was there to play the violin.

One of the heartbreaking stories from the sinking of the Titanic was that the band continued to play as the ship sank. I could only imagine what went through their minds as they watched the tragedy unfold. The horrifying realization that more would die that night than live.

They didn't ask to be in that situation. They didn't ask to have such a fate. But they decided to create music with the time that they had left.

Music that's believed to have kept people calm. A calmness that potentially prevented mass panic, which would've taken even more lives. The musicians used their last moments for something bigger than themselves.

"I want to make us Solo Tour jackets for this year too," said Stella. "We had so much shit happen last year. We deserve an easier Solo Tour."

I kissed Salem countless times on the forehead as I tried to say goodbye for the night. The previous nights at the hospital—kissing his forehead, not knowing if that was the last time I'd ever do that—was burned into my brain.

I didn't ask to be on that sinking ship, but I was going to play my heart out—so help me God.

I crawled into bed thinking of the tale of the starfish that one of my professors shared in class that fall semester—the same class that I'd documented my self-care for: a storm washes thousands of starfish onto the beach, one night. In the morning, a man sees a boy picking up and throwing starfish back into the ocean.

"It's useless!" the man shouts. "There are too many of them! It won't make a difference!"

The boy pauses, picks up a starfish, and throws it in the ocean.

THE YEAR OF DATING MYSELF

"It made a difference to that one."

Heal yourself. Build yourself up. Then use that newfound strength to make the world a better place, however you can. Even if it's just for one starfish.

Even if all you do that night is make sure a cat knows how loved he is.

I pulled my covers up, the exhaustion finally hitting me. Before I turned out the lights, I took my phone, opened my notes app, and began to type:

Plans for this year's Solo Tour . . .

Afterword / Acknowledgements

I first and foremost want to thank you, the reader, for following my journey of self-dating. I can only hope that, at minimum, some part of my story has motivated you to go on more solo adventures, step outside of your comfort zone, or do the incredibly scary act of loving yourself (as well as all past versions of yourself).

It is with a fully broken heart that I share with you that my beloved Salem passed away two months after he came home from the veterinary hospital. He'd been valiantly fighting cancer for the third time when he started having strokes. The doctors said that there was nothing more we could do but make him comfortable. Since he wasn't in pain, we decided to hold vigil for him until he either passed away naturally or it was time for compassionate euthanasia.

The last week of Salem's life was possibly one of the hardest times of my life. He didn't want to go, and his fight to stay was a testament to the grand spirit that lived inside that tiny body. He ultimately passed away naturally in Gabe's arms while I stroked his forehead and sang to him. By that point, he was so weak that his purr was little more than a vibration, but his purr was there until the very end, lasting even longer than his heartbeat. He left his earth knowing just how loved he was, and, in the end, that is all I could've reasonably asked for.

I write this afterword with tears so heavy I can barely see my laptop screen. To this day, the grief is overwhelming. Pet death is one of the most underrecognized forms of grief, despite it being one of the hardest. Anyone who has loved and raised an animal knows the hole that their absence leaves behind.

THE YEAR OF DATING MYSELF

This is why the very first people I want to thank are the incredible people who work at the Massachusetts Veterinary Referral Hospital, particularly those who work in the oncology, ICU, and ER departments. Your tireless work, expertise, and care are why I got that extra time with my baby boy. There will never be enough words for me to fully describe my gratitude.

I also want to thank my incredible support system—the people who have been constants in my life, even when I was at my lowest. No person is an island, and without your love I would've already drowned.

A huge thank you to my agent Rachelle Gardner, whose enthusiasm in my work breathed new life into an old dream. Thank you for your unrelenting faith in my writing, your honest feedback, your sense of humor, and your kind spirit.

I also want to give a huge thank you to my editor, Ashley Calvano, whose enthusiastic advocacy for my memoir was apparent from day one—and another thank you to Start Publishing, as a whole. Thank you for seeing what this book could do and giving it a chance.

Another huge thank you goes to my beta readers, whose insight when this was still a rough draft helped shape the book to what it is today. I want to thank, in particular, Sofia, Zara, Isaac, Shawn, and Aida, whose advice, suggestions, and commentary have proved to be particularly invaluable.

Another thank you to Ashley, Casey, Trista, Karyn, Jess, Shawn, and Epsilon. I don't know where I'd be without your love and support. To Isaac, thank you for steadfastly being in my corner since the beginning. I am who I am today thanks, in large part, to you.

To those who told me that they started going on more solo adventures because of my journey, thank you. There is something additionally healing when you know your climb back to the surface has motivated others to do the same.

I also want to thank all my graduate school professors, whose passion for teaching is what made my master's program such an incredible experience. While most identifying details about my classes were removed from the memoir, I'm sure a few of you could point out which classes I referenced.

(Likewise, I wouldn't be too surprised if at least some of you could tell something was going on in my life while I was attending your classes—and, if that's the case, thank you for not making it apparent to me.)

And a thank you to Milo and Artemis, my two other fur babies and Salem's younger siblings. Thank you for the pure love and joy you bring into my life. I see Salem's legacy in the way both of you move about the world. Thank you for the reminder that our time with our pets is devastatingly brief, but, without a doubt, worth it.

Lastly, Massachusetts Veterinary Referral Hospital is accepting donations in Salem's name for those who cannot afford the expensive chemotherapy treatments for their four-legged beloveds. I consider myself lucky beyond measure that we had the financial means to fund Salem's fight against cancer, but most don't have that luck. If you have any money to spare, please consider making a donation.

About the Author

Abby Rosmarin's professional writing career began when she became a writer for *Thought Catalog* in 2014, but Abby has been writing since she was a child. "Author" has been the one consistent job title in a sea of professional change. Throughout her life, Abby has been a teacher, a commercial model, a fitness instructor, and a behavioral health specialist.

Abby's work has appeared in a variety of places, including *Thought Catalog* (obviously), *HuffPost*, *Bustle*, *EliteDaily*, *xoJane*, *The Bangalore Review*, *Elephant Journal*, and more. Her essay "A To-Do List for Myself After My Father's Death" was a featured piece on *HuffPost* and translated into multiple languages.

She is also the author of seven books, including the Amazon bestselling *The Ballerina's Guide to Boxing*. While always a thrill-seeking Bostonian at heart, lately Abby has been happily living a quieter life in northern New England.

www.ingramcontent.com/pod-product-compliance
Lightning Source LLC
Chambersburg PA
CBHW010542230725
29937CB00004B/116